1·25

AND YOU VISITED ME

A True Story of Death Row Friendships

Penny M. Wheat
with Jan Greenough

MONARCH
B O O K S

Oxford, UK & Grand Rapids, Michigan, USA

First published in 2005 by Monarch Books
(a publishing imprint of Lion Hudson plc),
Mayfield House, 256 Banbury Road, Oxford OX2 7DH.
Tel: +44 (0) 1865 302750   Fax: +44 (0) 1865 302757
Email: monarch@lionhudson.com
www.lionhudson.com

Distributed by:
UK: Marston Book Services Ltd, PO Box 269,
Abingdon, Oxon OX14 4YN;
USA: Kregel Publications, PO Box 2607,
Grand Rapids, Michigan 49501.

ISBN-13: 978-1-85424-682-0 (UK)
ISBN-10: 1-85424-682-8 (UK)
ISBN-13: 978-0-8254-6084-5 (USA)
ISBN-10: 0-8254-6084-0 (USA)

Unless otherwise stated, Scripture quotations are
taken from the New English Bible.
Published by Oxford University Press.
All rights reserved.
pp. 54–55 "Kyrie Eleison" by Jodi Page Clark:
adm. by worshiptogether.com songs excl. UK & Europe,
adm by Kingsway Music. tym@kingsway.co.uk.
Used by permission.
In quotations from prisoners' letters, the original
spelling has been retained.

British Library Cataloguing Data
A catalogue record for this book is available
from the British Library.

Book design and production for the publishers by Lion Hudson plc.
Printed in Great Britain.

Contents

	Acknowledgements	4
	Foreword	5
1.	Dead End	7
2.	Family Life	10
3.	Making Contact	23
4.	New Friends	33
5.	LifeLines	43
6.	Searching for Honesty	56
7.	First Visit	71
8.	Divorce	85
9.	Travels in America	92
10.	Execution and Reprieve	106
11.	Understanding Anger	117
12.	Not Just a Number	127
13.	A Prisoner in Zambia	137
14.	Travelling Together	145
15.	Prison Life	154
16.	Debating the Death Penalty	168
17.	Giving and Receiving	179
18.	The Waiting Room	188
	Useful Addresses	191

Acknowledgements

I was hungry and you fed me, thirsty and you gave me a drink; I was a stranger and you received me into your house, naked and you clothed me; I was sick and you took care of me, in prison and you visited me. (Matthew 25:35–37, Good News Bible)

My thanks go to: Colin, for his unfailing love and support, and the many cups of tea he provided; Martin Elkes and his co-workers at Stafford Library, for assistance with research; Ann and Roger Venables, Colin Wade and Richard Curtis, my "techno-team" who patiently strive to bring me into the computer age; Brian Shaw for information from the family archives; Lucy Newill for her encouragement; Mary Nordkvelle, a dear and faithful friend both to me and many prisoners beside; Jan Arriens, for the foreword; my pastor, John Marshall, for his advice and for coming up with the book title; Jan Greenough, for her sympathetic editing; Monarch Books, who thought the story worthy of the telling; and last, but by no means least, to all my "friends inside", without whom there would be no story.

For reasons of confidentiality a number of names in this narrative have been changed.

Foreword

Penny has written a book that is remarkable for its honesty and integrity. It vividly brings out the way in which certain people can be deeply touched by the plight of prisoners, and also the difficulties and rewards of corresponding with someone under sentence of death.

I first met Penny when we both appeared on the television programme in Bristol which she mentions in the book. This was early on in her friendship with Tommy on Death Row. As she says in the book, her feelings for him began to move beyond those of ordinary friendship. In the television programme, she movingly described how she felt she had met her other half and hoped eventually to marry him, even though she had not been looking for a relationship and was at that stage still married.

It was, remarkably, Tommy who held firm and cautioned against romantic involvement. Here was a man with so little in his life and facing state-sanctioned death, who nevertheless backed away from what he must have wanted almost more than anything else. Time proved him right. Penny has remarried and her friendship with Tommy has moved on to a different plane again. When she visits him, her husband comes with her and has developed a relationship of his own with Tommy.

Penny's dilemma was one faced by a significant number of women corresponding with prisoners under sentence of death. The combination of a needy man and compassionate woman is a potentially explosive one. Romantic involvement in these circumstances can, however, lead to intense and distressing complications. Like Penny, I have seen women in the UK who have married their pen pals in prison, only for the relationship to come to grief. Penny's story shows the rich depths that such a relationship can achieve if both parties are prepared to work through the initial romantic impulses, however strong these may be. True friendship lies at a deeper level and is often intensely rewarding.

What her story shows too is just how much people supposedly on the scrapheap of society have to offer the outside world. Like many correspondents in LifeLines, Penny feels that we gain much more than the prisoners. As she puts it, "they had somehow retained their imagination, their warmth, and their interest in the outside world. They were tremendously alive." And through it all she is aware of a divine presence, right there in the misery. In Tommy's words, "God's right here in the thick of our day-to-day lives."

Jan Arriens
April 2005

1

Dead End

THE TYRES CRUNCHED ON THE GRAVEL as I reversed the hire car off the car park. Changing gear, I pulled away from the house that had been my home on all eleven trips I'd made to Tennessee. The modest single-storey house, in the poorest part of town, was owned by a Christian charity called "Reconciliation". It offered a safe and affordable place to stay for anyone visiting friends or family in Nashville's prisons. The same foundation also supported prisoners' children, so often the forgotten victims of their parents' crimes, organizing activities and parties to overcome their sense of isolation.

It was a drive I'd done dozens of times before. On either side of the main street stood dull clapboard houses, all painted a uniform blue-grey colour, with their rough grassed yards surrounded with steel chain-link fencing. From time to time there was a small business, with faded signs advertising liquor or Cajun food. After the boarded-up convenience store came the tall chimney of the fuel depot, with its constant plume of smoke. You could see that smoke from the inter-state ramp, several miles away, and when I spotted it on my way from the airport on every trip, I knew I had arrived.

Turn left at the lights, passing the petrol station and the timber yard; now the road was potholed, and the car splashed through puddles of water. There were criss-cross signs on both sides, warning of the railway crossing, and the wheels bumped over the narrow, unguarded railway tracks. Then, as I took the bend, the most extraordinary building came into view. It looked like a fantasy castle built of Victorian brick, with red roofs and extravagant turrets: The Walls, Tennessee's old prison. It had been closed in the 1980s, and was now hired out to Hollywood producers as a film set.

After the old prison the road widened out, with huge green signs on either side announcing the access to the inter-states, southbound and northbound. More lights, slung high overhead – red. I stopped the car at the cross-roads. Ahead were more landmarks: the water tower and single-storey buildings of the medium security prison, Middle Tennessee Reception Centre, with the initials MTRC in huge black letters on the side of the tower. Only another mile or so to go.

Now the road narrowed, and the poor housing gave way to modern industrial units. No pavements here, for no one walks – everyone working here comes by car. Then the buildings come to an end, and all around there are fields. The Cumberland river runs at the foot of the rolling hills to the left, invisible from the road where I drove, the car bouncing over holes patched roughly with asphalt.

As usual, I was struck by the incongruity of the scene. The landscape was beautiful in the pale February sun-shine, the fields peaceful and still. In the summer, crickets and cicadas keep up their tireless chirruping and hawks soar above in the hot, still air. In the autumn, the hills burn with tones of gold and red. It was such a desirable spot, you could imagine a property developer choosing the site for an estate of executive homes. That was when the black-and-white sign caught my eye, just one among the usual clutter of signs that line every American high-way. "Dead End".

Why hadn't I noticed it before? Surely it wasn't new?

The significance of the two words slowly registered on me. "There's nowhere else to go. There's no future for anyone who finds himself here. There's no way out. At the end of this road is death."

I wasn't being fanciful. Dead End was exactly the right description for this road, for many of the men who came this way into Tennessee's other prison. I turned left through an impressive stone gateway, and drove on up the drive between signs indicating the routes for delivery vehicles and the way to the visitors' car park, and warnings about searches for violation of regulations, and prosecution for misconduct. Weaving between the tall gantries, whose searchlights flood the whole compound with brilliant light after dusk, I pulled into a designated visitor space on the front row of the car park.

There in front of me were the low, buff-grey buildings, surrounded by high razor-wire fences. The prison complex sprawled across the compound, its blank solidity punctuated here and there with narrow, darkened window-slits. The grounds were immaculate, with neatly-trimmed grass and weed-free flower beds; it could have been a prosperous business or well-run office. I left the car and walked towards the main entrance, aware in the silence that the only sound was the smack, smack of the lanyards on the flagpole by the front door, where the stars and stripes flew bravely. I stepped onto the doormat, bearing the motto of the State Seal, and entered Riverbend, the Tennessee Maximum Security Facility – the prison that houses Death Row.

2

Family Life

I T ALL BEGAN IN THE SPRING of 1983, when I took my small daughters to the library to borrow some picture books for them. Just inside the door was a trolley where all the aged, dog-eared or unwanted books were placed to be sold off. If you wanted to know how to care for a gerbil, or where to fish in Scotland, or which gardens were open to the public in 1976, this was the place for you. Of course, there was also a stack of Mills and Boon romances.

Among the battered romantic fiction and the ripped cowboy adventures, one title caught my eye: *Who Killed Hanratty?* by Paul Foot. I knew Paul Foot was an investigative journalist – but I seemed to recognize the other name too. I'm the sort of person who always believes fact to be stranger and more interesting than fiction, and prefers real-life drama to the inventions of a creative mind, so I was immediately intrigued. I turned to the blurb inside the cover, and my memory was refreshed.

"Hanratty" was James Hanratty, one of the last people to be hanged in Great Britain. He was convicted of what became known as "the A6 murder" – the murder of Michael Grigson, and the frenzied attack on Valerie Storey, his girlfriend, which left her paralysed – and died at the hands of the state in 1964.

Inside the book's front cover was scribbled the price – 50p. I fumbled fruitlessly in my pocket for some change, but I had come out with only my library ticket. I had to have this book! I pushed it well to the back of the shelf and rushed home, hoping that no one else would buy it. I was back in record time with my purse.

I found it compulsive reading. I'm a fairly slow reader, and it was full of careful, detailed reasoning, but I could not put it down. Foot was convinced that Hanratty had been the victim of a miscarriage of justice. In fact, recent DNA tests on Hanratty's remains appear to support the original verdict – but whatever the truth turned out to be, that book was important to me. For the first time in my life I encountered the possibility that the law was not infallible, and juries could make mistakes.

At the back of the book was a series of letters, written from prison by Hanratty to his mother. It was heart-rending to read the successive messages that passed between son and mother, as time ran out for them. I was moved to tears, and surprised by the strength of my reaction to the story. That book was a turning-point in my life, which up until then had been wholly unremarkable.

I was an only child: my mother had been a college secretary, my father the deputy headmaster of a junior school. From him I inherited my love of art, literature and music – he had a wonderful bass voice, and could have been a professional singer. He had a lively and creative mind, and encouraged the same in me, taking me to art galleries and amusing me by quoting poetry and Stanley Holloway monologues, to my great delight.

Mum and Dad had attended the same school and started courting at a family party. They married in 1938, and I was born ten years later. My parents had a rock-solid marriage, but I never remember any displays of affection between them, no kisses or cuddles in my presence. Both came from rather strict families (my father's were staunch Methodists who had all signed the pledge) who disapproved of overt shows of emotion. They were determined that although I was an only child, I should not be spoilt; I never recall being praised much or fussed over. Certainly they never crowed about my achievements, even when I passed the eleven-plus and won a place at Brownhills High School for Girls, probably the best girls' grammar school in the locality. When I saw the pride with which some of my friends' parents spoke about them, I sometimes felt deeply hurt by my parents' apparent indifference.

At the age of eighteen I went on to college and studied for five years to gain my arts degree. I left as a qualified silversmith and art teacher, and immediately secured a job in a middle school in Leicestershire. Even then, I was still painfully shy – after a childhood spent mainly with adults (my parents and Gran, who lived nearby) and seven years in a single-sex school, I was self-conscious and awkward with boys. I'd met my only serious boyfriend at college, and we planned to get married, but he broke off our engagement. I understood why: we had serious difficulties. For one thing, his family were Roman Catholics, and they put pressure on me to convert to Catholicism. My background was Methodist and Salvationist, and though I tried hard to understand the instruction I was given, the more I studied, the more I knew I wasn't cut out to be a Catholic. At the same time, my father was dying of lung disease, and the stress of this caused me to become more and more impatient with my fiancé, causing endless arguments.

I had a few other boyfriends after this, but no serious relationships until I met Ian when I was on teaching practice. Ian was eight years older than me, and in the process of leaving an unhappy marriage; he seemed as unsure and diffident as I was, and we formed an instant rapport. We married in 1972, and started our life together in a tiny semi-detached house near Leicester, with both of us teaching in schools nearby.

One major development in our life together came when I was twenty-five: we both became Christians and were confirmed into the Church of England. As a child I had attended Sunday school at the local Methodist chapel, even though Mum and Dad – once regulars at Mount Tabor Chapel in Tunstall – had stopped going to church for some reason. They never made me go to Sunday school: I decided for myself that it would be a good idea. Perhaps, as an only child living in a neighbourhood where there were few other children around, I wanted the chance to mix with others of my own age. However, I think I always had an interest in spiritual things. Perhaps I was unconsciously searching for an added dimension to my life. Ian was the eldest of three children of a church minister, so he too had been raised in a Christian home, though he hadn't attended church as an adult.

We didn't realize that we were both looking for some meaning in our lives until we were invited by Jim, a vicar friend of mine, to join a trip to Manchester to see the film *Jesus Christ Superstar*. The film was not essentially Christian: it presented Christ not as a living and resurrected saviour, but rather as a good man who suffered from delusions. Nevertheless, it made a deep impression on us both. For the first time, Jesus the man became a reality to me. He was no longer a fictional character from a story written thousands of years ago, or even a historical figure who lived so long ago that he was no longer relevant. Now he stepped right off the screen and into my consciousness. As a child I had accepted that Jesus was the Son of God, but he seemed remote and unapproachable; now his humanity and vulnerability hit me, and I dared to believe that he had walked this earth and shared our experiences.

I needed the assurance of faith. My marriage to Ian had got off to a shaky start – even our honeymoon was not the romantic adventure I had anticipated. Ian's divorce settlement had left him with nothing, and we were on a tight budget, so I felt twinges of guilt every time we spent any money. Things began to go badly wrong from day one. As a result, even in those early days I was suffering from mild depression. One Saturday afternoon, shortly after the Manchester trip, I was alone in the house, and in floods of tears. I couldn't understand why I felt so low: newly married, with a job I loved, my life should have been happy. Through my tears I cried out to God for help, and suddenly, in my mind, I heard that still, small voice saying, "Peace". I felt an overwhelming sense of calm, as if I was washed all over and cleansed.

Later on, I often wondered about that moment's experience. Some people say that humanity invented God as an emotional prop – and I certainly needed a prop at that time. Maybe it was nothing but the invention of a distraught mind, or the effects of medication. Yet I have never been able to escape from the love that surrounded me at that moment, nor deny that it was a dramatic and life-changing experience.

Ian and I began to travel the twelve miles or so to worship at Jim's church two or three times a week, and he and his wife Mary became dear friends. Jim had a fine mind, and we had stimulating debates on religious topics, with him quoting from the original Greek of the New Testament. We were impressed with the practicality of their faith: with four young daughters to raise, they had little enough for themselves, but I never knew a tramp to be turned away from their door empty-handed. Whatever time of day I called, there was always a warm welcome – a tea towel or a potato peeler would be thrust into my hand, with an invitation to help prepare a meal and share it with the family. They taught me the value of Christian hospitality and acceptance.

Under their kindly tuition, my faith began to grow, and to support me in my various personal disappointments and troubles. Being part of a strong community helped too. Ian and I were both sad that because he was a divorcee, we had been denied a church wedding: Jim laid on a special service of blessing for us, and Mary organized a small party at the vicarage.

Shortly after this, Mary was diagnosed with terminal cancer, and after her death, Jim moved to a new parish. With both our friends gone, there seemed little point in travelling so far to church, so we moved to our local church in Stone, where we enrolled for a study course called The Bishop's Certificate. It was a major commitment – a meeting every Monday evening in term time for two years – and an exhaustive syllabus, covering Bible history, textual study and social, historical and political background. Our parish priest was a stimulating group leader, so we had plenty of thought-provoking and informative sessions to keep us engrossed.

I revelled in this opportunity to explore my faith, and became more and more involved in church life, as a member of the parochial church council, a deanery synod representative, youth fellowship leader and church magazine illustrator. Thanks to the vicar's promotion of my talents, I secured a contract to produce a series of drawings for Mowbray, the religious publishers, and several other small commissions followed as a result.

After his conversion, Ian had hoped to follow his father into the full-time ministry, but his divorce and remarriage were a stumbling block as far as the Church of England was concerned. He decided instead to study for the lay ministry, on a new course which involved a great deal of study, written work and practical application. Alongside his teaching career, it kept him very busy indeed for four years. It struck me as ironic and farcical that when the church was short-staffed it was Ian who returned home from holiday to help out at a wedding service. Many of the young couples who wanted a "proper" wedding, with all the trimmings and ceremony of a religious service, had never been inside a church since their baptism, and they were ill at ease and unfamiliar with the conventions. I often wondered if the spiritual aspect meant anything at all to them, and whether the church was doing itself a disservice by agreeing to marry people who simply wanted to use the building as a splendid backdrop for their photographs. I lacked the grace to understand how often God uses such occasions to plant a seed which may bear fruit in someone's life years later. He is able to use any opportunity to draw men and women to him.

I didn't want to appear intolerant or judgemental when I myself had been won over to Christ by the total acceptance of other Christians, but the situation made me uneasy. Ian could not be remarried in church, nor could he be ordained as a full-time priest, but the church was happy enough to use his services for free. He often conducted three services on Christmas Day, and every weekend he preached in local churches and farther afield. At the same time, upheaval in the education world meant that teachers were being made redundant, and Ian decided to improve his status by enrolling for a degree course at the Open University. His free time was totally absorbed, and we hardly ever saw him.

By this time we had a family: Frances Helen arrived in June 1975, and Hilary Anne followed two years later. Having children was important to us, and though Frances' birth was difficult and traumatic, and she was not an easy baby, we had been determined that she should not be an only child. Hilary had many health problems from birth, but fortunately she had a calmer temperament than her older sister. By the time Alison Ruth was born in October

1980, I felt that I was shouldering all the family responsibilities. I was always tired, feeling that life was one long chore, and my isolation and desperation grew. Ian had an ever-increasing work-load as head of year in a middle school, with responsibilities for pastoral care, plus his lay work and his studies.

One of our house moves typified our situation: with no car, and unable to afford a removal firm, we shifted everything ourselves in a hired van, feeding babies and changing nappies as we went! I felt badly let down by our Christian family, only one of whom came to help us. However, even as I brooded on this, I began to appreciate how frustrated and let down God must feel all the time – we so often fail to support each other as he would want us to. It's so important to grasp that we are a family, and that we should be aware of each other's needs. I realized how many small acts of kindness I had failed to do over the years, and how often I had failed the test myself. It was a challenge to do better.

We had moved house initially to be nearer my mum, but we did so during a slump in the housing market, and lost money on the deal. Money was a constant worry, and everything seemed to make the problem worse. Ian had been treated for Hodgkins disease, a form of lymphatic cancer which had claimed the life of his father when he was eight, and this meant that our mortgage insurance was unreasonably expensive. There was never any spare cash for treats. I didn't drink and I had never been much of a socializer, but I did enjoy dancing and the occasional theatre visit. There was no money (or time) for any of this. I began to feel bored, and then guilty about being bored. Married life was not living up to my expectations, and Ian seemed to be as daunted by our problems as I was. He wasn't the dynamic person I had thought was hiding behind the shy façade. His poor health had other repercussions for us too, and the physical side of our marriage began to fall apart.

I had married a good man, who was honest and faithful, but he didn't make me happy, and I don't think I made him happy either. I felt lonely, miserable and trapped. I had prayed every day of my married life that things would improve, but they never did, and I felt betrayed by God. Christians are not promised a life free of trouble, but I did believe that as Christians we should stand a better than average chance of forming a solid relationship, with God's help. Disillusionment set in, and I knew I was growing cold and hostile. How could I witness to others when my own life was in such a mess?

To me, divorce was not an option. No one in my family had ever been divorced, and even the thought of it filled me with shame. I had married for life, and that was how it should be. After all, my husband wasn't a wife-beater, a drinker, a gambler or a philanderer, so what was my problem? Anyway, it would be an admission of failure, and I *hated* failure. I prided myself on my stamina, my problem-solving abilities and my stickability. Not for me the fly-by-night attitudes of the current generation, who gave up on relationships at the first sign of trouble.

TV programmes seemed to reflect the current lack of application and fidelity: there was a whole raft of popular messages on the subject. "Everyone is entitled to be happy"; "Nobody should stay in an unfulfilling relationship"; "People don't have to stay together for the sake of appearances"; "Women today are more financially secure and independent than in the past"; "It's not good for children to see their parents at war." I wasn't convinced. What about responsibilities? Marriage needed to be worked at. As followers of Christ, we are warned that we each have a cross to bear, but we are also promised a helping hand and strength beyond our own.

I was bound by emotional shackles as strong as any physical ones: my moral outrage at the thought of a failed marriage, my sense of duty towards my spouse, my concern for my mother's conservative views, and my worry about the effect on my children. Quite simply, I could see no way out of my predicament. Many nights I lay awake in the early hours, unable to sleep, my mind racing. Sometimes I went downstairs and wept. Ian was concerned, but he didn't know how to comfort me – he seemed paralysed by my unhappiness.

The longer we were married, the harder it became to break away. Financially, of course, we held everything in common, but the emotional ties were even stronger. I despised myself for my dependence, but still I hung on, hoping and praying that things would get better. I even began to wonder about divine retribution. I was familiar with passages in the New Testament which stated that second marriages were adulterous, and the partners sinners. I had married a divorcee – was our union doomed from the start? We tried counselling, both secular and Christian, acutely aware of the disintegrating and ever more destructive nature of our relationship, but by then, there was little left to salvage.

As a silversmith I was teaching part-time, with hours that fitted around the children's needs – first at Stafford College, and later at Newcastle College too. I added some private tuition in English and basic maths in the evenings to supplement our income, but there were still too many lonely hours to fill each day. I joined the International Pen Friends Association, and gained friends all around the world – in Australia, Austria, Germany and Holland, writing to them regularly. I loved receiving letters from all these different people, and hearing about their very different ways of life.

Then the local paper announced that they wanted

someone to write a regular cricket column, and advertised for readers to send in a sample report. Cricket has always been one of my passions – Dad started it, listening to the old Bakelite wireless set with the sunburst design on the front. One of my abiding memories of childhood summer days is the sound of John Arlott's voice delivering the cricket commentary, drifting through the open window of our house as I played in the garden. Throughout my teens I had followed the local team, which was lucky enough to have Sir Gary Sobers, the cricketing legend, as its professional.

I sent in my report, signed with my initials, and was rewarded by a telephone call: it was the (female) editor, asking to speak to "P. M. Morgan". "That's me," I said. She was surprised to find that the writer was a woman, but agreed that this was unforgivably sexist!

I began writing a weekly column. The work was unpaid, but it had the bonus of a press card for me, giving me access to the press box at Lord's for several big matches, in the exalted company of other "proper" commentators and journalists. I enjoyed sitting there with my notebook and pencil, while around me the others, all men, tapped busily away on their laptops, downloading their reports direct to their news editors.

At this time I was living a very settled, ordinary life, and I came from a very stable background. All the same, I think an interest in social justice ran in the family. Those staunch Methodist forebears, for all their unbending manner, had an acute social conscience. In the 1880s they took in a bargee's child, nine-year-old Rhoda Blackhurst, when her parents abandoned her on the towpath (apparently a common occurrence when the family grew too large for the barge). They brought Rhoda up as their own, and after her marriage she and her children continued to be regarded as part of our extended family – it was only after my mother's death that I discovered the documents which indicated that some of my "cousins" were not actually blood relations at all.

We were a respectable, law-abiding family, who knew only other respectable, law-abiding citizens. I was never taught to be judgemental, but there was a prevailing belief in our home that people in jail deserved to be there, and that the police were doing a good job. I had grown up with a quiet certainty that safeguards existed in the judicial system to prevent innocent people from falling through the net and paying the ultimate penalty. When I found Paul Foot's book in the library that day, and read it so carefully at home, I began to reassess that opinion.

I became aware of several high-profile cases of miscarriages of justice. My cosy little world was rocked hard by the realization that the law wasn't foolproof, and neither were the people implementing it. I felt as though someone had pulled out a tin from the bottom of the pile, and now the whole stack was teetering precariously.

The cases of the Birmingham Six and the Guildford Four were in the news at this time (all were later proved to have been wrongly convicted of pub bombings in 1974). So, too, was the case of the Bridgewater Three: there were actually four men – Jim Robinson, Pat Molloy, and Vincent and Michael Hickey – who were convicted of killing a paper boy, Carl Bridgewater, in 1978, but by the time they were released, Pat Molloy had died in prison. I joined the campaign to have their cases reopened, and wrote letters to the Home Secretary on their behalf. I even wrote to Michael Hickey, who had staged a roof-top protest in Gartree prison, enduring eighty-nine days of bitter weather to draw public attention to his case. He wrote back to me, saying that he had lost all faith in the criminal justice system, and that he believed that the pressure of public opinion was the only thing which would ultimately come to his aid.

My interest was enlivened by a BBC series called *Rough Justice*, which highlighted such miscarriages of justice, and which based its programmes on material provided by "Justice", a law reform group. I joined the organization and began writing to MPs and the Home Office about each case featured; I even took friends carol-singing to raise funds for their work.

I learned that justice, far from being the application of common sense, or the search for truth, was often little more than a mind game between opposing factions, with each lawyer trying to outwit and score points off the other, exploiting legal loopholes and points of order. The majesty of the law had been devalued somewhere along the line. It had lost its integrity, and it seemed that most people hadn't noticed.

This new interest, together with my work, my campaigning on environmental issues, my letter-writing and my cricket column all helped me. I was trying to keep busy and fill my days with some sort of creative and useful activity to make up for the intense loneliness I experienced in my marriage. It was a welcome diversion from my own troubles, though I still fought a constant battle with my old enemy, depression. I especially liked the contact with the local paper, and the feeling of being in touch with local affairs. Perhaps it was a combination of these things that made me take such an interest in the case of a local man – a man who had committed a horrific murder and then attempted to commit suicide.

3

Making Contact

PETER'S CASE HIT THE HEADLINES in 1982. A local man from Stafford, he had drowned his two young sons and then attempted to take his own life. The papers were full of morbid details and vilifying comment. His daughter had found him, barely alive, in a bath full of blood: he had slit his wrists. The children were beyond help, their lifeless bodies carefully laid out on a bed. He was transferred to hospital, but while the police were waiting to interview him about the boys' deaths, he made a further attempt to kill himself by jumping from a window. He failed in this attempt too, but sustained some serious injuries.

The horrific details of the case provided the local reporters with plenty of gruesome copy, with scope for stirring up every emotion from anger to morbid curiosity. There was a break in the coverage while the case was prepared, and then it returned to the headlines during his trial and subsequent conviction.

The more I read, the more sickened I became: not just by the all-too-graphic descriptions which inevitably appeared in print, but by the attitudes of those reporting on them, and also by the popular preconceptions and prejudices of the ordinary folk of my home county. Try as I might, I couldn't put the case out of my mind. Twice a week, on my way to work, I would pass the "house of horror" where it all took place. Each time, a mental image of the man and his unfortunate children came into my mind. What had those little boys suffered? What about the ongoing trauma of the man's daughter? It got so bad that I was beginning to wake in the night, not in fear, but with a feeling of great sadness. I was haunted by one question: what could have driven Peter to do such a thing?

I knew about depression from my own experience, and I had a certain morbid fascination with the idea of suicide: I had even thought about it myself, on occasion. I had come to the conclusion that it was an act of great cruelty to the rest of the family. Those left behind would be shocked and traumatized; they would feel helpless, and at the same time guilty for not having realized how bad the situation was. I had rejected suicide as a way out of my problems, because I didn't want to hurt the children (though at my lowest points, I confess that I might have wanted to hurt Ian). Also, I felt I could never attempt it if I wasn't 100 per cent certain that I would succeed. How terrible to gather your courage to make that final decision, and then to be resuscitated – to find that the pain which drove you to this act was going to continue. I felt faintly envious of people who succeeded in committing suicide, and thus brought their own pain and loneliness to a conclusive end, even though I knew they were selfish to use this method to punish the loved ones who had let them down.

However, even more perplexing to me was the fact that Peter had killed his children. I simply couldn't think what could have made him do that. I had small children of my own, and though I knew parenthood wasn't all plain sailing, it had so much joy and happiness in it that I couldn't imagine what had brought him to such desperation. Children give you hope for the future, even when your own life seems entirely black and hopeless. You want to be there always to support them, to see their first day at school, their sports day, their face when they open their birthday presents. Everyone looks ahead to those land-marks – how could Peter have blocked out all that? Someone, I thought, should do something. Someone should try to find out why.

Weeks passed, but the idea persisted, and a small voice in my head began to nag. "*You* do it. Don't expect anyone else to. This one is down to you."

I tried to ignore it. I told myself I was mad, mistaken. How could I talk to a convicted prisoner? I'd never even stepped inside a prison, let alone spoken to a double mur-derer. Several days passed. More broken nights. More questions. Still I resisted. The voice got louder and more insistent, the nights more disturbed. In despair, I gave in, and spent a whole morning ringing all the local firms of solicitors, trying to find out who had represented Peter in court, and what had become of him since his sentencing. I drew a blank everywhere.

As a last resort, I telephoned the newspaper whose arti-cles had so appalled me. I didn't expect to be told anything of use, since I had no connection with the case, but they were able to tell me the name of the prison where he had been sent. A quick look at the map and a search through the Liverpool telephone directory at the library, and I had the information I sought.

I thought it might be best to approach Peter via the prison chaplain, so I wrote a letter explaining that I had taken an interest because the crime had happened in my locality, and I was disturbed by the adverse publicity and hostility it had evoked. While condemning the act itself, I found I was unable to condemn the perpetrator, and won-dered if he felt able to share with me what had gone so terribly wrong as to cause him to do such a thing. I kept it fairly short, but I did mention that I felt compelled to write, and wished to appease the "demon" in my head which kept badgering me so mercilessly.

I posted my letter with a mixture of relief and apprehension. What had I done? Suppose I got a reply? Had I really written in expectation of one? It was too late to worry. A reply came, not from the Anglican chaplain but the Catholic one. Peter was a Roman Catholic, and so the letter had been passed on to Father Alfred. He explained that Peter had broken several bones in his leap from the window, but he had been shown my note, and said that he would like to respond when his injuries allowed. This was to be the beginning of an unlikely friendship, which lasted three years until Peter's death in 1985.

I was very nervous the first time I went to Liverpool to meet him. I had quickly learned the rigmarole of applying for a visiting order, and found out what could and could not be brought for an inmate and handed over to the prison officers. I drove up the M6 and made my way to Walton Jail, Liverpool. I don't know what I expected – I could hardly believe that I had got involved and was actually doing this. How would I recognize him? The newspapers had carried pictures of him being hurried into a police car with a blanket over his head, so I had never seen his face. I had plenty of time to ponder on this. The hospital wing was reached by walking what seemed to be miles from one end of the prison complex to the other, accompanied by a prison officer.

The room was dreary, with a high ceiling, in typical Victorian work-house style, but the only signs of incarceration were the heavy iron bars at the windows, which looked out across a dismal yard at more buildings. Otherwise it was just like any other hospital ward. Several men were sitting around, watching TV or talking. I wondered if Peter was among them, but there was no one to ask – the prison officer had disappeared, leaving me alone in the ward. Then a small, bespectacled, rather unprepossessing figure limped towards me from a side room, and I knew this was Peter. He was still suffering the effects of his fall, and his ankle had yet to heal fully – but it was his mental condition which worried me more.

He began by telling me of his childhood in a poor Glasgow home, his migration south in search of work, the failure of his marriage and the ensuing liaison with the mother of his two little boys. Everything had gone tragically wrong. First he lost his job with a builder, when the construction industry suffered a slump. Then his common-law wife walked out on him, taking his beloved boys with her. He spoke of his fears for the toddlers, believing that they were being neglected and physically abused in their new home. One weekend they arrived for a visit with no spare nappies, feeding bottles or baby food, and both boys had bruises. Peter was almost out of his mind with worry. He notified social services about his anxiety for the children's welfare, and waited for some action to be taken, growing more impatient with each passing week. In a cruel twist of fate, it was revealed in the press that the social worker had made a note of his concerns, and the case had been earmarked for investigation during the week after the tragedy took place.

As Peter described his feelings of anger and helplessness, I began to understand the tortured reasoning that had caused him to take the boys' lives and try to take his own. He didn't want the children to return to their mother; somehow, he thought that in death he would never be parted from them again. He was convinced that the three of them could be together in heaven.

Peter was a fascinating person. He had little formal education but he had read widely, especially political history, and in the weeks that followed we had many interesting discussions. I usually visited with the family; Ian would often wait outside in the car, but I took the girls in with me. I had no doubt that Peter had truly adored his own two sons, and I wanted to show him that I trusted him with my own children. I also wanted the girls to see another, less sheltered side of life: I didn't want them to grow up as I had, completely naïve about people who had committed crimes. Anyway, he was by now a good and valued friend, so it was only natural that my family should meet him, as they did all my other friends.

The last time I saw him, he had been moved to Rainhill Secure Unit, Merseyside, where he shared a block with eleven other men and women similarly detained under the Mental Health Act – all described formally as "criminally insane". It was not a description that immediately sprang to mind when talking to Peter: he was delighted to see us, treated us with his customary courtesy, and gave me a big bear-hug when we left. All the same, I was concerned about him. He seemed to have improved very little, and he was unwilling to take his prescribed medication. His behaviour was obsessive, and all he could think about was his boys. I was filled with a deep unease, and asked him (as I did on each visit) to promise not to harm himself.

I received a final letter from him, apologizing for not having written for a while – he had broken the knuckles of his right hand and was having difficulty holding a pen. Referring to the press coverage his case had attracted, he wrote:

> I'm beyond hurt but I feel terrible for my family who do not deserve all this but it's done now. I'm hoping to be released next month sometime and I will certainly drop you a line Penny. This letter is to thank you and Ian also my lovely three little friends Fran, Hilary and Alison for your friendship all through this ... I shall always be indebted to you and I'm very happy to have got to know you as I find you very special and I hope someday I shall

be able to befriend someone in the manner you
befriended me. Please convey my gratitude to everyone
Penny and tell them all I shall never forget what they
done for me … thanks a million for everything.

In retrospect, it was obviously a "goodbye" letter, though
this wasn't apparent to me at the time. I had been right to
worry about his mental state. Several weeks later I had a
phone call from the police. Peter had been released, and
had committed suicide shortly afterwards. He had
drowned in a disused quarry.

I was distraught – what a terrible, lonely way to die.
The police rang me because they knew from the prison
authorities that I had been visiting him, and they asked
me several questions, including whether I thought he
should have been released. I had to say that I did not – I
knew he was troubled, and he was always talking about
going to be with his boys, and not being separated from
them any more. It was clear what he had in mind, and I
had feared for his safety.

At church we had set up a prayer partnership scheme,
and the other two members of my "triplet" came with me
to Peter's funeral at Stafford crematorium. I knew from
what Peter had told me that his daughter had never come
to terms with the trauma of finding him after his first suicide attempt. The rift between them had never been
healed, much to his distress. It all seemed so sad, so point-
less. Why had my friendship not been of more help to
him? Had I failed him utterly? Had I made any difference
to him at all?

It took me a long time to work through my feelings
about his death. I missed him as a friend, and I felt a deep
sense of failure – yet I came to see that whatever my effect
on Peter (and I had his letters to reassure me that he had
appreciated my friendship too), he had had a profound

effect on me. Knowing him had changed me so much. I understood for the first time that people who commit even the most horrific crimes are not necessarily inhuman monsters, but people who have been swept away by circumstances they have been unable to control, and have resorted to acts which are unthinkable for the rest of us. Peter had many failings, many weaknesses, but in his own mind he was acting reasonably in response to what was for him unbearable pain.

I still had many questions. Why had my attempts to show friendship and concern been so inadequate? Had there been any point in striking up a friendship with him? I wished desperately that I had been able to prevent his death. Nevertheless I felt a deep assurance that our meeting was meant to be, and that a bigger scheme of things was in operation. Whatever the purpose, and however poorly equipped I was for this particular ministry, it had changed my life.

It was around a year before I felt ready to befriend another prisoner; I had a natural reluctance to get hurt again. However, when I reread Peter's letters, it was clear that although I had not made any difference to the final outcome for him, my friendship had cheered his lonely months in prison. Perhaps I could do the same for others. I launched into several new correspondences in quick succession.

Most of these were short-term prisoners: one was a young woman in Droitwich who had smothered her baby son; another was a man from St Albans, miles from his home and family in my local jail and badly in need of a visitor. One young man persistently stole food and clothing from his old school, where Ian taught. When he discovered that it was Ian's coat and credit card he had stolen, he wrote to apologize, saying that Ian was the only teacher he had liked, and who had seemed to have time

for him. He returned everything and asked for our forgiveness. We had already cancelled the credit card, of
course, but we were delighted to receive his apology; we
kept in touch until his release. To his great credit, he managed to keep out of trouble after that, and settled down to
raise a family of his own.

Dave wasn't in prison, but he heard about me through
the Justice organization. Dave was sure he was being
harassed by the police. They had organized a heavy-
handed night-time raid on his home, and accused him
(falsely, he said) of a fairly minor crime. He was desperate
to get them off his back.

I visited him at home, with some information that I
thought might be useful to him. "Home" turned out to be
a dreary bed-sit of the poorest kind, and unbelievably
untidy, with clothes strewn everywhere and dishes piled
up in the sink. Dave offered me a seat, but I had to clear
it of a pile of stuff before I could sit down. Then he offered
me a cup of coffee. I looked at the dirty, chipped crockery,
and my stomach turned, but I knew I had to accept. My
fussiness about hygiene had to take second place if I
wanted to offer him my friendship and support.

Several friends at church knew about what I was
doing, and the Mothers' Union invited me to go on their
speaking panel. I travelled all over the Lichfield diocese,
speaking to church groups about my experiences of visiting prisons and the friends I had made. Then the chaplain
at the local women's prison invited me to give a talk there,
and afterwards several of the girls came up for a chat. As
a result I began writing to Chris regularly, and once a
month I would drive over to Drake Hall on Sunday afternoon to visit her. Chris loved jewellery, and always sported
a pair of exotic-looking earrings. As a silversmith I spent
a lot of my time teaching students how to make jewellery,
so I loved to see what she was wearing for my visit, and

we often discussed her wonderful collection of weird and dangly creations. Chris was a very intelligent and articulate girl, who expressed herself well in her letters. I wondered how someone so accomplished and educated had fallen foul of the law.

I always felt it was a privilege to be able to share in these people's situations and to be given their trust. Whatever small kindness I was able to give them, they always repaid a hundredfold, and my life was enriched by knowing them. I had always been a bit of a maverick, never caring much what other people thought of me, and never courting popularity. I was a loner, and my friends were often those whom no one else bothered with. I always found myself siding with the villain, not the hero of novels and TV plays. Now I was meeting so many different people, all with a different tale to tell. Perhaps it was no wonder I could relate to the outcasts, who ended up on the wrong side of the law.

4

New Friends

WHEN YOU ARE PAINFULLY SHY, letter-writing is a good way to increase your circle of friends without having to manage face-to-face meetings. These days, with the proliferation of electronic means of communication, it has become something of a lost art. How much easier and speedier to send a fax, an email or a text message! Yet not everyone has access to these – especially not in prison – and besides, a hand-written letter shows a degree of thought and consideration not found in a hastily dashed-off, impersonal email. Receiving a letter through the post is one of life's great pleasures, and you can read and reread it later at leisure.

Today, even after receiving many hundreds of letters, the rattle of the letterbox and the sight of the envelope lying on the mat still give me a thrill. Every letter is kept and treasured; they are all carefully sorted into bundles fastened with elastic bands, and stored in shoe boxes. Each person who has bothered to respond is there in my collection, and can be brought to mind in an instant: their faces, their characters, and the ups and downs of the lives they have shared with me. Each one is a special friend from whom I have learned so much, and whom under different circumstances I might never have known.

People always ask, "What do you write?" as if people in prison were from a different planet, with different needs and interests. I reply that I write as I would to anyone:

normal, everyday stuff about job, home, family and holidays. I don't avoid describing holidays to people who are locked away, for if I did I would be contributing to their isolation, helping to diminish their world and shrink their horizons. For the period of their sentence, they can live outside through us, and their spirits can be liberated when their imaginations see through our eyes. I've never been aware of jealousy, resentment or negativity on their part: only a generosity of spirit, a delight in sharing, and satisfaction in being included in someone else's life.

Another common question is, "How do you get in touch with people?" Generally speaking, I don't find them, they find me. Peter was different – I admit that I sought him out – but since then I have mostly been given names by contacts who knew of my interest and someone else's need.

In this way I continued to make contact with prisoners whenever the opportunity arose. To supplement our income I was giving private tuition at home in English and basic maths, and one of my pupils was Leon, the son of a prison officer. Leon was a bright boy but he was struggling with his school work. After a couple of sessions with him I came to the conclusion that he was dyslexic, and persuaded Ken, his father, to arrange a proper diagnostic assessment. (At that time dyslexia was a little-known condition, and some parts of the educational establishment did not even believe it existed.) The diagnosis was positive, and Leon's parents were relieved and glad to have an explanation for his difficulties and the opportunity to get proper help for him.

It was Ken who told me about Terry. Because Terry was a Mancunian, he had first been remanded in Strangeways until his trial; after his conviction he was sent to Stafford jail (a dispersal prison where men are kept before being allocated a place elsewhere to serve out their sentence), and eventually moved on to Featherstone, near Wolverhampton. Ken was a senior prison officer at Stafford, and he had read the case notes and spoken to Terry and his brother Des, who was also in his charge. He had formed a liking for the boy, and he had some misgivings about his conviction: it seemed possible that he had been falsely accused by his girlfriend.

"He badly needs his faith in the female of the species restoring," said Ken. "I know you're interested in prisoners' welfare. Would you write to him?"

I replied that I was happy to take Terry on as a pen-pal, but I needed to hear from him that he would like to have me as a correspondent. Confirmation arrived almost immediately.

Dear Penny,
Hello, thanks very much for your letter, I was quite surprised at receiving it so soon because it was only a short time ago that I spoke to Mr —— on the phone, asking me would I like a pen-pal, he mentioned your name during our conversation and I said yes I'd like a pen-pal, I honestly didn't think I'd receive your letter so quickly, but I am pleased that I did. By the sound of your letter Penny you lead quite an active life with all the things you do, as you probably know prison life isnt what you call exiting but I do have interests in a few things, some I can do while Im in here and obviously some I cant, well Penny to start with my outside interests are cinema, fishing, walking, riding my motorbike and supporting my football team, now dont laugh Penny, I support Bolton Wanderers, what do you mean who are they, have you stopped laughing yet Penny?

Terry had a wonderful sense of humour, and was especially fond of dreaming up crazy book titles. One of his best was *"Rusty Bedsprings* by I.P. Knightly". It became customary for us to exchange one or two at the end of each of our letters. His brother Des was quite a character too:

> Dear Penny and Co,
> Hi. My name is Des. Im Tel's big bro. Terry told me all about you and what have ya. He speaks very highly about yas. He asked my permission to let yous know a little about myself. I told him I don't mind as long as it's all good! Ha! ha! Only joking Pen! So I said I'd drop you a few lines myself to say hello and thank you myself for writing to him and being his pen-pal.

He went on to add: "He shouldn't even be in prison. He's in for a crime he didn't commit, he's innocent. Im the guilty one, not of his crime but my own."

In true supermarket fashion, I had got myself a two-for-the-price-of-one deal with the two brothers!

Terry was always interested in what we were doing, and liked getting postcards when we went away.

> Cheers for your letter, I received it Friday, I was quite sur-prised to receive it so soon, coz with you being so busy I was expecting it sometime after the weekend, many thanks Penny anyway. I also received your postcard you sent me from Greece, it came on Thursday the 9th, the place you went to looks nice in the picture, is it just as nice when you actually see it as the picture shows?

As I had been warned, he had serious problems with trust, and it was naturally very hard for him to come to terms with his incarceration, which he believed to be unjust. In one of those early letters I described my appearance, and asked him to paint a word picture of himself.

A little question Penny how come you asked me for a description of myself in great detail? Is it so you would recognise me if you visited me? About visiting Penny, yes I would like a visit with you, that way we could possibly get to know each other a bit more or should I say abit better. Im not being chauvanistic or nasty Penny it's just that I trust *no one*, especially females, its through a females *actions* that I got sent to prison, lie after lie and I end up in prison ... my trust went to zero rating and I doubt if I will ever trust anybody ever again, in here Ive got no one to talk to about my conviction except my brother, but I want to talk to somebody independent who's not a judge, jury and executioner ... you say in your letter that when I feel a bit more comfortable with you I could possibly talk to you about it, has Mr —— not mentioned to you what my conviction was ... or should I call it a miscarriage of justice because thats what it is, yes Penny I would like to talk to you about it but I don't know you yet, Im duebius about talking about it with you because after we've spoke you'll probably have the same response as everybody else has done and blank me out and end our newly found friendship, which I dont want to happen, I dont know how you will repond but after you know the truth the choice is up to you love ... are you a Christian Penny? The reason Im asking is because you mentioned going to church in your letter, I became a born again Christian on January 2nd this year and was blessed by Neil Proctor (senior chaplain) while I was in Strangeways on remand, have you heard of Neil Proctor Penny? Believe me he is a saint, although I dont go to church here Ive not lost my faith, even after all the things that have happened Im still convinced that God is watching over me and that only he knows my destiny.

Building that fragile trust takes time and patience. Despite his inner turmoil, Tel was a joy to visit, and usually one of the girls would accompany me on my trips to

Featherstone every six weeks or so. "Dear Penny ... thanks very much for the visit love, it was good seeing you and Hilary for the very first time, I just hope it wont be the last love because I realy did look forward to and also enjoyed our visit together."

In a later letter headed "Featherstone Loony Bin" in typical Tel manner, he was still cautious about our relationship, and displayed unease about a query I had raised:

> Our Des asked me to tell you thanks a million for his birthday card, he was quite chuffed about recieving it coz he wasnt expecting one off youse ... anyway love as for your little question about me getting 4 years for a first conviction, I seem to detect that you might not believe me that Ive got no previous convictions, I say with all truth love that Ive none whatsoever and as for the 4 years Im stumped to why that judge give me such a steep sentence for a first conviction, mind you Penny the judge who sentenced me is getting quite a reputation as a hard judge, I call him send them down Sachs.

To add to his anguish, Tel's dad died while he was in prison, on the same date as my own father had died some years previously: 6 January. Tel had requested a home visit to see his mum.

> Well love Ive been granted my home leave in March but the dates Ive asked for havent been confirmed yet, Ive asked for the 11th to the 14th March because as you already know its mothers day on the 13th March and before me dad died he said to mum if he lasts long enough he will take her for a meal on mothers day, but sadly he didnt make it as you know. so me and Des have promised mum that we will fullfill dad's promise.

His worries were further compounded when his mother was admitted to hospital suffering from an angina attack. For some reason, having our fathers die on the same date brought Tel closer to me, and he started to call me his "big sis", and to sign off his letters to me "little bro Tel". The girls adored him, and referred to him as "Uncle Tel".

Visits to Tel were always entertaining, because he retained his irrepressible sense of humour in spite of all his problems. One day he pointed out another young prisoner, who he said had been apprehended for a robbery. He giggled as he described the man's perplexity at having been caught so speedily. "The cops checked the details of the getaway car on the DVLC computer, and traced it straight back to him! The idiot used his *own* car to commit the crime!"

He also enjoyed a joke at our expense. The WRVS ran a small coffee bar for the benefit of inmates and their visitors, and one day Hilary was volunteered to join the queue for coffee for the three of us. Behind her in the queue was a tall shambling figure of a man, around sixty years of age. When Hilary returned with the tea tray, Tel said to her, "Did you notice that chap behind you in the queue? He and his wife are in for child murder!" The expression of horror on Hil's face had us in fits of laughter.

A short time later Des was released at the end of his sentence, and Tel was transferred to an open prison near Wetherby, Yorkshire. He was able to work in the fields surrounding the facility, growing vegetables, and lived in a dormitory in a single-storey, barracks-like building, with fifteen other men. He had several home leaves and weekend furloughs, and was hoping for parole when he received bad news.

Im sorry I havent written sooner but since Monday the 14th my head has been in bits. The parole board knocked back my parole ... the parole board said the reason they refused me an early release was Mr — has resisted all attempts of confronting the offence and until he does so, he will be an unquantifiable risk, in other words Penny, because I wont admit to it there not releasing me early.

The female probation officer's report had helped form this decision, and of course this confirmed all Tel's harsh views on women, which we had been trying so hard to dispel.

She is supposed to be helping me, not cause me to stop in jail for a further $7^1/2$ months, because of her I wont be released until July of next year now, Im sure you must understand how Im feeling Penny, I want to blow my top but I cant, people keep telling me I must trust woman more, how the hell can I do that when one put me in jail and one wants to keep me in jail ... because I pleaded not guilty I must be a very high risk. It gets better Penny, I received a letter off her today (Thur) saying she has just recieved the decision of the parole board people and she understands that Im upset about the decision, she also understands why Im blaming her for it ... she might as well have put a gun to my head and pulled the b— trigger ... sorry about this letter sis, love to Hils and Al, write soon, take care and God bless all my love Terryxxxxxxxx

In a letter headed "Lunatic Asylum and Mind Destroying Institute" he told me of the governor's decision to put his home leave on hold until he had completed a course:

... either an *anger control course* or an *alcohol awareness course* or an *offending behaviour course* in other words Penny I do what he tells me to or its no home leave, what he is doing is blatent blackmail ... Ive agreed to go on the anger control course *but* under protest. I refused to go on any of them at first because by doing so *it* in my mind is addmitting the nasty conviction *But* the probation in here re-assured me that by going on the anger control course is *not* an admission of guilt it is to help me in the future *not* to get into the position again which inevitably got me into prison, I hope you can understand that Penny coz its all balderdash to me.

Tel completed the course and was allowed his home leave. He gained his parole next time around, and we kept in touch for quite a while, exchanging Christmas and birthday cards and the occasional phone call. He brought his frail elderly mother down from Bolton to visit us: she was a sweet, gentle lady, who gave me a pot plant and thanked me for my friendship with her boy. After that I received Christmas cards from her too.

How on earth had all this come about? When I sent off those first, nervous few lines to Peter, I never dreamed of the journey on which I had unwittingly embarked: I never imagined that it would lead to a lifelong involvement with captives. It's probably just as well, for I might have been scared off. Fortunately God in his wisdom shows us only as much of the big picture as we can handle at the time. Our understanding is so limited, and our vision so parochial, that we often fail to see the invisible thread which he weaves into the tapestry of our lives.

For now we see through a glass, darkly; but then face to face: now I know in part; but then shall I know even as also I am known. (I Corinthians 13:12, Authorised Version)

It's odd how we can go through life with set ideas and preconceptions, until one day something happens to overturn them, and shake us from our prejudice. Like many others, I suspect, I had a notion of what men and women in prison were like. Without knowing it, I was judgemental and bigoted, and it was only when I met people and got to know them as individuals that I came to know differently. I believed in the rule of law, the desirability of an orderly society, and the personal responsibility of the individual. Knowing Peter taught me to balance this with the knowledge that not everyone has the same experiences in life, the same stable family background, the same chances, the same educational opportunities. Life is not a level playing field.

I am not soft on crime or criminals, and I don't seek to excuse bad behaviour. However, I do believe that everyone is a child of God, made in his image, and that this has serious implications for us all. It is a challenge to Christians to seek out the good in our fellow men and women, and the search can be costly, in time, effort, money and emotions. It can be a challenge to the criminals too. Often they come from homes where little or nothing is expected of them, and where failure in the world's eyes is almost built in. When we see them through God's eyes, we can show them other possibilities. We can tell them, "You are precious in God's sight. You can do better, be better. In his name, I expect better of you. Don't be afraid to try and fail, because we all do that every day. Only be afraid to fail to try. Ask his help daily. He is faithful and won't let you down, as mortals do."

For fourteen years I had written to and visited men and women in English institutions. I was an experienced prison visitor, confident now, and perhaps even a little smug. But all that was about to change.

5
LifeLines

MY CONTACTS WITH PRISONERS meant that I continued to take an interest in all aspects of the criminal justice system, and over a period of about five years my thinking began to focus on one specific issue: capital punishment.

In the United Kingdom the death penalty was abolished in 1964; when the House of Commons reaffirmed the Act in 1973, it described capital punishment as "inhuman and degrading". Most democratic countries share this view: around eighty countries worldwide have abolished the death penalty, including Canada, Australia, New Zealand, almost all of Europe and much of Latin America. However, almost as many countries still use capital punishment, with the highest numbers of executions being carried out in China, Iran, the United States, Vietnam and Singapore.

It was a television programme which first drew my attention. *Fourteen Days in May* told the true story of Edward Earl Johnson, a young black man who was executed in Parchman Penitentiary, Mississippi, in 1987. It was movingly told: Johnson was extremely likeable, and his death was unwelcome to everyone around him, including the prison staff. Yet the wheels of "justice" rolled inexorably onwards to their sad conclusion. Watching this documentary brought back all the feelings I had when I first read Paul Foot's book about Hanratty. There were doubts about the safety of Johnson's conviction, and I cannot imagine anything worse than the state taking the life of an innocent man.

I felt that such doubts deserved the closest possible scrutiny, yet once Johnson was convicted there seemed to the viewer to be only one possible outcome: execution. This seemed to me to bring the law into contempt, make a mockery of the pursuit of truth and honesty, and rock the foundations of society. What purpose was there in trying to build a civilized democracy when so many people's questions could be ignored, just for the sake of political expediency? In a democracy the crown or state acts on our behalf, thus we share the responsibility for such mistakes. If we sit back meekly and accept such killings, we are acting like Pontius Pilate, washing our hands of the deed.

My emotions were stirred. I was concerned that the states with the Death Penalty were killing their citizens in as premeditated a way as any cold-blooded murderer, and might not always show sufficient concern about whether or not the executed one was the guilty one. It was as though the issue of guilt had somehow been subsumed by the necessity to kill *someone*, anyone, as a response to the horror of the crime; in some vaguely Old Testament manner, the idea of the scapegoat. "For thou desirest not sacrifice; else would I give it: thou delightest not in burnt offering" (Psalm 51:16, Authorised Version). "Your burnt offerings are not acceptable, nor your sacrifices sweet unto me" (Jeremiah 6:20, Authorised Version). "In burnt offerings and sacrifices for sin thou hast had no pleasure" (Hebrews 10:6, Authorised Version).

Formerly I had been the sort of person who supported the death penalty without question, thinking that we needed a strong deterrent for increasing crime, and believing that the system contained adequate safeguards to protect the innocent. Now I was not so sure that capital punishment worked as a deterrent, and I had grave doubts about the reliability of the law in bringing the right person to justice. My views had changed radically and irrevocably. I hadn't become a softy: I still believed in punishment, and indeed, I considered some of the sentencing I read about in the newspapers to be derisory. The punishment should fit the crime – but it should always stop short of execution.

My experiences of prison visiting in this country also influenced my thinking. I was greatly disquieted about the way we treat our antisocial element, not least because I now had personal friends on the other side of the legal fence. I knew them to be people of worth. None of my views was clear-cut any more; answers were not so simple; solutions were not so obvious. I had turned into a firm believer in rehabilitation, education and counselling for offenders – very little of which exists in either the British or American penal systems. I suppose this was why I felt I ought to be personally involved with people in jail, in the hope that such contact might make a difference to someone's life. In the event, the life it made a difference to was mine.

Two other television programmes gave me an insight into the situation in the United States. *The Execution Protocol* was a chilling description of the science of human extermination. It showed how the process of killing people had been sanitized so that those taking part were able to distance themselves from the dreadful reality of their actions. Each procedure was carefully designed to be clean, impersonal, efficient and infallible, in theory at least, and all in order to protect the sensibilities of the execution squad. I was nauseated.

The second programme was in the BBC *Everyman* series, and told the story of Ray Clark, a prisoner on Florida's Death Row, and Mary Grayson, a middle-aged piano teacher. Mary began writing to Ray after seeing an advertisement asking for pen-friends for men in US jails.

Only eleven letters were exchanged in the months before Ray's execution, but a strong trust and friendship quickly developed between them. Although on the surface the middle-class musician had little in common with the jailbird, they had somehow contrived to delve below the surface and tap into each other's real humanity. Looking back on the broadcast now, I think I may have unwittingly been envious of that strong, deep, personal relationship. I longed to share in a friendship of such intensity.

At the end of the programme an address was given for the LifeLines organization. This group, based in Cambridge, aimed to put prospective writers in touch with men on Death Row across the United States – men like Ray Clark. Thousands of viewers must have had the same reaction as me, because LifeLines was overwhelmed by the numbers applying to be pen-friends, and a tiny group of volunteers struggled to cope with the resulting mail.

I have since tried to analyse my response to that documentary. Partly it was the natural development of my thinking so far, about the nature of punishment, the needs of the ordinary men and women who committed crimes and found themselves isolated and in prison, and the cruelty of the death penalty and the associated condition of the men who spent years on Death Row. Yet there was a more personal aspect too. I was certainly lonely in my personal life. Perhaps I was searching for the kind of openness and intimacy that Mary and Ray had developed; perhaps I even wanted to be needed by someone who relied on me for his emotional support. Maybe I was looking for "safe" involvement – with a person who was separated from me by great physical distance and kept in a secure environment, who could make no real demands on me. Maybe I was looking for someone who would make me feel good about myself. I don't know. At any rate, I wrote off to LifeLines and waited in eager anticipation.

A few days later a large envelope arrived, containing a letter and an information pack, which I was asked to read very carefully. I was impressed by the degree of thought and care which had gone into this. It spelled out clearly all the possible drawbacks, complications and problems which might arise from corresponding with a man under sentence of death, and even gave a list of contacts to advise in case of difficulties. At the end of all this was a plea that if I was in any doubt about any of this, or of my suitability as a friend for someone in this situation, I should go no further. LifeLines was anxious to ensure that vulnerable men were not trifled with; all friendships should be seen through to the end. No prisoner should ever have cause to regret beginning a correspondence with a "LifeLiner".

I was pleased with the idea that the men's welfare was paramount, and as I signed the form promising that I would abide by the rules, I felt as if I was signing a legal and binding contract. I returned the form, along with a note explaining that I had previous experience with prison friendships. I was accepted.

The LifeLines pack suggested that writers should first send a short note on the back of a colourful postcard: the men liked to have cards to brighten up their cells, and a card gave just enough space for a few words of introduction. I wrote to the first name I was given – Darrell – but received no reply. I applied for another contact, and wrote a second postcard, this time to Charles. After three months I had still received no reply, but I was convinced that eventually I would get lucky. I decided to write off for name number three, but before I had time to do so, a letter with a US postmark dropped onto my doormat. It was from someone I'd never heard of – Tommy.

In my card to Darrell, I had suggested that if he didn't want to write to me, he should pass my details on to someone else, and he had given the card to Tommy. Charles, my second contact, already had a pen-friend; Tommy had put my card away and forgotten about it. That was why I had heard nothing for so long. Then, one day, as he was searching for some of his legal papers, the card had fluttered down off the shelf. At first he was reluctant to write, but later changed his mind:

> ... thinking it certainly would be interesting to correspond with someone from another country. I don't think Darrell likes to write letters often and your letter does state if he decided not to write back would he pass it on to someone who does ... several guys here have been receiving letters from people in your country ... I have been here for ten years now, fighting for my life and I really appreciate the many people around the world and in this country who voice their opposition to the death penalty.

I couldn't wait to get to know Tommy, and find out about the circumstances that had led to his desperate situation. However, in my usual contrary fashion, I hoped and prayed that he was a guilty man.

My reasoning was this: I knew how many miscarriages of justice there had been in Britain, when men had been imprisoned for long periods of time, only to have their convictions overturned on appeal, either because the original evidence was found to be unreliable, or because new evidence had emerged to prove their innocence. No system could give those men back the years they had lost in prison, but at least their freedom could be restored to them. There was no reason to suppose that justice in the United States was any more reliable, but once someone had been executed, there was no going back. When I heard of various miscarriages of justice, like the case of Edward Earl Johnson, I felt a deep sense of pain, impotence, anger and betrayal. I didn't think I could bear it if I befriended a man who was innocent, and had to go through those feelings again, but on a more personal level of intimacy and involvement. No, better by far if my man was guilty.

People have often asked me, "How can you make friends with someone who may be guilty of the most horrendous crime?" I always answer that I am there just to be a friend. I have never asked for details of the offence before taking someone on: if the prisoner wishes to share such details with me, I am there to listen. Otherwise it doesn't concern me.

From time to time stories appear in the press about young, impressionable girls who write to notorious killers and sometimes even marry them. Such stories worry me, and I wonder about the girls' motivation. Do they get a salacious thrill at the thought of the grisly murder their friend has committed? Do they have such low self-esteem that they feel they cannot get a boyfriend any other way? Or do they somehow imagine that they have the power to "redeem" such a man? Personally speaking, I wasn't seeking sensation. I wasn't looking for a dark, satanic character who would horrify me with tales of his gruesome deeds. I just wanted someone I could relate to at some level.

It's worth stating at the outset that most men on Death Row are not mass murderers like Ted Bundy or Richard Ramirez, and their crimes are not glamorous or exciting, in spite of their image in Hollywood films. Most are men who come from poor, deprived and often abusive backgrounds, and who have been caught up in circumstances which spiralled out of control. A disproportionate number of them are black. Most of them are too poor to afford their own legal representation, so they have been defended by court-appointed attorneys who may be poorly qualified and ineffectual: many prisoners spend a great deal of their time doing research for their own appeals.

Tommy told me outright that he had been responsible

for a man's death, which he deeply regretted. This was a huge relief to me. He did add that he had acted in self-defence, believing his own life to be in danger when a gun was pulled on him. A struggle had ensued, and the victim was shot with his own weapon. Tommy signed off his first letter:

> I hope I wrote your address correctly on the envelope because I've never written to anyone in another country before now. I also hope we will open a line of communication and friendship in the near future and I'll certainly be waiting to hear from you soon if you choose to do so. Take good care, and best wishes, Tommy.

In his next letter he told me a little of his own case:

> Once society labels a person's behaviour intolerable and he falls through the cracks of our criminal justice system in receiving the ultimate sentence, he is often looked upon as some kind of homicidal psychopath and while I am indeed in the midst of a few men who are genuine sociopaths and borderline maniacs, it would be a mistake to throw a blanket indictment over everyone who comes through a prison door as being a cold-blooded killer or mass murderer.

He added how regrettable was the loss of any life, and what deep remorse he felt for his own part in the taking of one, but added that the real reason he found himself in his current unenviable situation was a failure of the criminal justice system. "Although a loss of life did occur on that unfortunate night, the fact that I was defending myself in a life or death struggle was obviously lost in the jury's decision. I killed him in self-defence, yet they made out I executed him."

Was he just saying this in order not to scare me off? I

knew he viewed me as a demure, middle-class English lady who lived in a land where the grim reality of capital punishment no longer existed, and perhaps he was anxious not to shock me. Perhaps these were exactly the excuses that any killer would use to justify his actions. Yet his words had a ring of truth. Was I being incredibly gullible?

He too had seen *Fourteen Days in May*, and believed Johnson to have been innocent. Expressing his deep revulsion of the death penalty, he conceded that it would be strange indeed if he were to hold any other opinion, but added that he had always thought that state-sanctioned killings were wrong. "I've always had trouble understanding how a State is able to kill a human being as setting an example to society that killing is wrong."

His interests were wide-ranging. We began to discuss politics, a subject in which we both had a great interest. He wanted to know all about Britain, our constitution, parliament and monarchy, testing me at times with his perceptive questions and making me painfully aware of my own ignorance of the legislative process.

He also told me about his day-to-day routine, and the way Tennessee's prisons operated. He was, he informed me, a Category A prisoner, which meant that he had earned maximum privileges by consistent good behaviour over a long period. He was allowed contact visits, so he did not have to sit in a cubicle behind a Plexiglas screen and speak via a telephone. He could also walk around the unit without wearing handcuffs and leg-irons, and he was one of just twenty or so inmates who had paid employment. They worked in a specially designed data processing unit on an outside contract for the Vehicle and Drivers Licensing Department. The system was mutually beneficial: the department paid much lower wages to the prisoners than they would have had to pay in the free world, but the prison gained considerable income it would not otherwise have had. However, it was all too easy to lose these privileges for some minor infraction of prison rules; when that happened, the prisoner had to work his way up through the levels all over again, over a period of some months. This carrot-and-stick approach was a useful tool for the prison authorities in maintaining order. Tommy had kept his Category A status throughout his incarceration.

> I'm basically a quiet sort of fellow compared to most of the hell-raisers in here. I respect others and expect the same but you know this is a maximum security prison and not a Sunday school camp. Even minor incidents are capable of escalating into bloodshed or worse in the blinking of an eye.

He always had plenty to say, for instance, on religion:

> What I need to know is not just that God exists beyond the brightness of the stars as some kind of cosmic intelligence who keeps the whole show going, but is there a God right here in the thick of our day-to-day lives, trying to get messages through our blindness as we move around down here knee-deep in the muck and misery and wonders of the world. It's not objective proof of God's existence I want, but the experience of God's presence.

I had got myself a philosopher! I wrote back and told him that I believed the fact that we had been put in touch with each other was proof enough, and for me it demonstrated God's work in our lives.

After we had been corresponding for a couple of months I asked Tommy to send a photo of himself, and promised to send one in return: "Exchanging photos will give us a vision to go along with our correspondence. I like that very much." When it arrived – a small prison Polaroid – he wrote:

I have never taken a very good photo as you can see but at least this shot will give you a vision of some sort … well Penny I can't wait to get a photograph of you also but I already know that you are one beautiful lady I am very lucky to become a friend of yours.

The snapshot showed a big man (Tommy was six foot two inches tall) sitting on a narrow bunk in the confines of a cramped cell; I could see a shelf on which stood a small television and other personal items. Neatly folded clothes were carefully stacked on another shelf. It was very tidy, but the cream walls were completely bare. Tommy explained that inmates were not allowed to put up posters, and could display photographs on their desks only. Tommy himself was muscular, middle-aged, bearded and black. He had long, thick hair and was wearing shades; he had a nice smile, but my first impression was of an ageing hippie. Not my type at all – pony tails on men were definitely not my style!

However, the more letters we exchanged, the more it appeared we had in common. He was almost the same age as me; his birthday was in May, like mine. Both of us were avid readers, interested in politics, current affairs, nature and sport. I asked him to send a list of the things he was allowed to receive: it wasn't long, but it included cassette tapes (an item which was withdrawn some time later), provided they were the see-through kind, so that they could be checked for drugs. We sent each other some of our favourite music – mostly nostalgic sounds of the sixties – and even recorded a few words of greeting to each other.

To begin with I spoke briefly on my tape to Tommy, but he was very coy about letting me hear his voice. He said his voice wasn't "refined" like mine – he described himself as having a voice like a "Mississippi bullfrog", and this became the nickname by which he was known. Actually I thought his rich, deep tones put me in mind of molasses. I told him I thought my voice sounded like the Princess Royal with a sore throat, so henceforth I was known as "Princess".

More tapes followed. He sent me "Reach Out" by the Four Tops, and I was instantly transported back to my college days. "I'll be there to love and comfort you. I'll be there to always see you through. Reach out ... " – wasn't that what LifeLines was all about? I responded with a Diana Ross song called "If we hold on together":

> If we hold on together
> I know our dreams will never die.
> Dreams see us through to forever ...

Though the grammar was suspect, the sentiments precisely matched my own; we were there to give each other support. No one could proscribe our hopes and dreams.

I have catholic tastes in music: Elgar, Delius, Warlock, Vaughan Williams, Brahms and Mozart, folk music and jazz – all are favourites of mine. At times of desolation, when God seems far away, I have always been able to lift my spirits by listening to a Christian song. One of my favourites is "Kyrie Eleison": the haunting, solemn tune is complemented by lovely words:

> Look around you, can you see:
> Times are troubled, people grieve?
> See the violence, feel the hardness
> All my people, weep with me.
> *Kyrie eleison, Christe eleison, Kyrie eleison*
>
> Walk among them, I'll go with you,
> Reach out to them with my hands:
> Suffer with me, and together

We will serve them, help them stand.
Kyrie eleison, Christe eleison, Kyrie eleison

Forgive us Father, hear our prayer:
We will walk with you anywhere –
Through your suffering, with forgiveness,
Take your life into the world.
*Kyrie eleison, Christe eleison, Kyrie eleison**

I used to imagine God speaking to me through the words of that particular song, bidding me go out to my various prisoner friends, to demonstrate his love and care and concern for them. Another favourite hymn is "My song is love unknown", the words of which always remind me that we are called to befriend everyone, prisoners and social outcasts included: "Love to the loveless shown, That they might lovely be." Unless we know that we are loved, we are unable to show love to others. So many of the people who end up embroiled in a life of crime come from damaged and difficult family backgrounds, where love is not always unconditionally given. God's love, however, is constant, eternal and dependable, and we are called to demonstrate this to others as best we can.

We may feel totally unfitted for this task, but the glorious fact is that we don't have to be perfect before he can use us for his work. If we step out in faith, he will equip us and use our inadequate efforts to do good. The Lord who took the loaves and fishes and used them to feed a multitude can take the meagre offering of our faith and multiply its power. We don't need to waste time worrying about the weakness of our faith. Even a weak faith can move mountains if it is faith in a strong God.

---

* Extract taken from the song "Kyrie Eleison" by Jodi Page Clark. Copyright © 1976 Celebration/Kingsway Music.

6

Searching for Honesty

I AM OFTEN ASKED WHAT MAKES PEOPLE like me write to a man on Death Row. I'm not entirely sure, but I think it's important to examine one's motivation honestly.

For most people, there is a certain fascination with men and women who kill – the popularity of crime novels and fictional TV programmes attests to that. The horror of true crime is undeniably exciting, and finding what drives a person to commit murder is of universal interest. To deny this macabre appeal would be less than truthful. As far as my relationship with my friend Tommy was concerned, did the fact that he was in prison fighting for his life add spice to the situation? Undoubtedly it did. Here was a man in an unimaginably grave position. The worse his outlook was, the more I wanted to help him.

However, this is only an initial reaction, and in my case at least there was much more to it. Some people thrive on the adrenalin rush of extreme sports; I am not one of them – the notion of putting myself in physical danger holds no appeal for me. But perhaps I got the same stimulus from taking emotional risks, by opening up my feelings to a friend who might be taken from me at any time.

On the other hand, the relationship wasn't as risky as all that: I was always free to walk away from it. Tommy was locked up securely, and far away; he wasn't in a position to make too many demands on me. In fact he was helpless, and totally reliant on my willingness to interact with him. Prisoners are literally a captive audience, and they desperately crave human contact which makes them feel valued. They are so used to being hated, feared and reviled that they respond eagerly to anyone who shows them any humanity. In a prison/free-world relationship, the partner on the outside has tremendous power over the emotions of the person on the inside, and such power can be hard to resist. Was this part of the attraction for me?

In my desire for honesty before God, I searched my motives mercilessly. When I began this life of correspondence all those years ago, I looked on it as a sort of mission. The lack of effective rehabilitation in our prisons means that many men will emerge, having served their sentences, more hardened and skilful criminals than they went in, with no inner resources or external support systems to help them reintegrate and become useful members of society. Because the system did not seem to try to confront, understand or change antisocial behaviour, I wondered if I could do anything. If my friendship and understanding affected just one man's attitudes, that would surely be a good thing. Perhaps one or two of my correspondents might be helped to discover some self-esteem and a sense of personal responsibility which might keep them out of trouble in the future.

Was I just being a "do-gooder"? It's a term people sometimes use to decry those of us with liberal tendencies, who refuse to see everything in simple black and white, who try to see both sides of a set of circumstances, or give another the benefit of the doubt. I must say that the people who use words like this usually have little compassion for or comprehension of the plight of other people. Yet surely we all want to do something worth while and positive to make a mark on society. No one sets out to do evil; and the alternative is to do nothing.

Ralph Chaplin, an American poet of the First World

War, wrote a remarkable poem called "Wobbly", about the struggle for workers' rights in the early part of the twentieth century. He wrote:

> Mourn not the dead
> But rather mourn the apathetic throng
> Who, cowed and meek
> Can see the world's great wrong
> But dare not speak.

At least the do-gooders are trying to speak out against wrong, and trying to improve the situation.

Of course, I am aware that some people feel that befriending prisoners amounts to condoning their crimes – as if total isolation from all normal human contact should be part of their punishment. They feel that anyone who helps prisoners has lost sight of the victims of their crimes.

It's true that no one close to me has ever been murdered; no doubt, if they were, I should be full of rage and hurt and vengeance. I thank God that I have not been tested in that way. He knows our limitations and will not press us beyond our endurance. However, I do know of two deaths in particular which have touched me. Hilda Murrell was an anti-nuclear campaigner and a Shropshire rose-grower – I recall seeing the sign bearing her family name hanging over the entrance to the nursery. Hilda was something of a kindred spirit: we were both passionate gardeners, artists, music lovers and campaigners. As an opponent of nuclear power for many years, I had written countless letters to lobby for the closure of the industry, as had Hilda. She was a woman of great determination and strong convictions: she had taught herself nuclear physics in order to be able to understand the issues and answer her critics. Her concern was for future generations, and her unselfishness touched me. She died in 1984, just before she was due to present a paper at the Sizewell inquiry. The circumstances of her death were later explored in a play called *Who Killed Hilda Murrell?*

A second death was that of Willie MacRae, a Glasgow lawyer. Willie was a leading light in the Scottish National Party and a fervent anti-nuclear campaigner. His unexplained death, almost a year to the day after Hilda's, bore striking resemblances to hers. These two were people I hugely admired, and I corresponded with a nephew of Hilda's and a friend of Willie's after their deaths. Thus I had another perspective, albeit at second hand, of the effects of violent death. I knew something of the strong emotions stirred up by such a loss.

I was also deeply affected by the film *In the People's Name*. This was based on the true story of a remarkable couple, the Murphys, whose daughter Jenny was brutally murdered by John Burke. In the film, after Burke's conviction, Jenny's mother campaigns tirelessly to ensure that the State of Colorado puts him to death, but over time her husband's views modify. He visits Burke in jail in Denver, and becomes even more uneasy about his execution. He persuades his wife to visit the man, and the film captures the harrowing occasion when they sit face to face for the first time and confront the reality of what Burke has done and the impact his actions have had on all their lives.

Burke also has one daughter, and pleads with the couple to take her into their home after his death, as there is no one else to care for the child. The film ends with him strapped to the gurney in the death chamber. Burke has asked Mrs Murphy to witness his end, to give her closure. As he lies there, in the final seconds, he mouths to her, "I'm sorry," and she mouths back, "I forgive you." The couple leave the prison with the young daughter of the man who killed their only child. It would be hard to imagine a finer example of forgiveness and reconciliation.

In the case of Tommy, forgiveness was not mine to offer; all I could hope to do was to offer him a "normal" relationship, by post, with someone on the outside. Becoming friends in this way meant sharing the stories of how we had become the people we were today.

Unlike most men in his situation, Tommy did not come from a broken home or suffer any form of child abuse. In fact, he described his childhood as "wonderful", and he obviously adored his family. He had not been involved with alcohol or drugs. Indeed, the more I learned of his background, the more surprised I was that he had ended up where he was, for apart from being black, he did not fit the normal profile of a man on Death Row.

He admitted that he always had his own agenda, trying to make a quick buck, being greedy and unwilling to wait for anything that took his fancy. In his youth he had fathered three children, and now he was a grandfather, and concerned about the welfare of his family. He tried to maintain contact with them all, and sent them whatever money he managed to earn, to buy Christmas and birthday presents. He often told me how he felt he had failed as a parent, and that he should be "out there" helping them, not languishing in prison.

Despite his loving and stable childhood, there had been a dark side to Tommy's upbringing, which probably accounted for his going off the rails. His own parents had been unable to look after him, his two brothers and his older sister. The children had been parcelled out to relatives, and Tommy and his brother Bernard went to live with an aunt and uncle, who had a boy and girl of their own. Tommy was devoted to this couple, and for several years he had believed that they were his real parents. He referred to his cousin Frances as his sister, and always spoke with great affection of the couple who took him in, and who treated their "adopted" boys like their own children.

This idyllic family life came to a shocking end: the parents were abducted and brutally murdered, their bodies burned beyond recognition. The reason was never known, though it seemed to be a mistaken act of retribution. Tommy was traumatized, and lashed out at everyone in anger and revenge. He was already gambling heavily and mixing with criminals, but now he became utterly reckless: "My life was completely without direction in those days Penny. I don't want to make any excuses for my past. There is no excuse ... but I do promise that I never knowingly harmed anyone innocent."

He had evidently struggled with the task of telling me about his past.

> I began this letter two days ago, but I kept rewriting it in trying to explain something that really has no explanation other than the plain old truth and mistakes I've made in life. I've had ten solid years to come to terms with myself and it's been a pretty long mind-bending process but hopefully things will get better and I'm able to dust myself off and pick up the pieces of my life.

I asked how he managed to keep so upbeat and cheerful, for every letter he wrote contained some small comment to make me smile: "In truth I have no option ... my sanity is about the only thing I have left intact after years of isolation and under threat of death." There followed a vivid description of the old prison where he had served the first seven years of his sentence.

> Inside of my old cell was so small that I could spread my arms and touch both sides of the wall. Can you imagine living several years in a room considerably smaller than your bathroom? It's no fun Penny, but you must stay

mentally strong to deal with it and the fact that you're just sitting there waiting to die is not much help either.

A federal judge had visited the old prison on a day when the temperature was well over 30°C – the prison had no air conditioning and the heat was exhausting – and ordered it to be closed. The new prison was hastily built a mile or so down the road, and the men rehoused. Tommy had mixed feelings about the move. The new place was better in terms of comfort and hygiene – there were no more cockroaches on the floors, no more bugs in the food – but socially the men's lives were poorer. At The Walls, the old prison, the visiting rules had been fairly relaxed, and in the summer months prisoners were even allowed to picnic with their families in the prison compound. At the new prison the rules were more stringent. It was an indication of the importance the prisoners attached to any human contact, that Tommy felt that improved cleanliness and comfortable temperatures were a poor trade-off for visiting rights.

As usual, he ended his note with a quip: "Well Penny, I guess I should bring this to a close now and prepare for supper. We are having 'mystery meat' again tonight which means your guess as to what it is will be as good as mine."

Movingly, he wrote that my letters had made him feel wanted, and added wryly, "Of course, I've felt wanted before but it was usually by some law enforcement agency so it doesn't count."

We touched on everything in our writings, without embarrassment, and were very comfortable with one another. I amused him by saying that I hated "pussy-footing around": "I haven't heard that expression for years! I guess we're both two pretty up-front, direct individuals."

We discussed politics, religion, sport, music, current affairs and personal matters. He was intelligent, thoughtful, well-informed and easy to talk to; whatever effort I put into the correspondence, he gave back a great deal in return. Though his body was confined, his mind and imagination roamed free. He kept up to date with world events by watching TV news channels and reading everything he could lay his hands on. He knew more about current political issues – not just American but global – than most people in the free world. I was impressed by his hunger for knowledge and his enquiring mind. He constantly pumped me for information, and had an insatiable desire for facts and figures.

Because of my environmental interests, we discussed the Earth Summit in Rio. He wrote:

> I remember a few years ago our news media referring to him [President Bush] as the environmental President but now that it is time for him to put up or shut up, he seem as out of place as a vegetarian in a meat market. It brings to mind a Horace Walpole epigram, "This world is a comedy to those who think and a tragedy to those who feel."

Corresponding with Tommy was stimulating and fun, but I still had plenty of time on my hands; I thought perhaps I might take on a second pen-friend. About six months after making contact with Tommy, I saw an advertisement in *The Wing of Friendship*, the LifeLines magazine, for volunteers to write to men serving life sentences in the USA. Apparently there were fewer people willing to write to men who were serving long prison sentences, but who were not on Death Row. Without that dramatic threat hanging over them, it seemed that they were less interesting; after all, there are plenty of long-term prisoners serving ordinary sentences here in our own country. I felt sorry for these lonely men, and offered to take one on; that was how I met José.

José was a Mexican American in a Californian jail, and he turned out to be a very helpful friend, as he was willing to help Hilary with her Spanish! He was also a very gifted artist, and often sent us beautiful, detailed drawings, painstakingly done in coloured ball-point or pencil. As soon as I became aware of his ability, I asked him to submit a drawing for a book of prisoners' artwork which a friend of mine was compiling.

I received a letter from the Rev Mary K as you said she would, and she did asked me for a drawing for her book, and right now I'm working on it, it is almost done, maybe by tomorrow. Although I don't believe I'm good enough for the book here's one for you: about hers I'm going to do my best, and hope is what she want. The one for you is not one of my best because I can't do faces as I mentioned. Next time I'm going to send some drawings for your daughters.

I asked for a photograph; he sent one from his foster-mother, Olympia.

This picture was taken in 1979. I don't even remember exactly when. I was hoping mom would send a recent one but I guess she could find another or she like this one. Nowadays I sport a mustache and my hair is straight back and weight ten more pounds ... now you can have an idea how I look.

His early life had been spent on the streets, scrounging food wherever he could find it; he admitted that he couldn't remember committing the crime for which he had been imprisoned, because he was under the influence of drugs at the time. He assured me, though, that he knew he was guilty.

You said that you've been involved with convicts, in various ways. I want you to know, is nice to know there is still some people out there who cares, someone who thinks we're humans, and like humans we make mistakes … I always wanted to do better, but I didn't have the same opportunities as the average person, for the simple fact that I wasn't born here, and as I was growing up I've lived foster homes, and the street, since I can remember. I meet my mom untill I was 15 years old. So you can imagine what kind of life I lived. Just to eke out a living I had to work harder … all kinds of odd jobs but most of them were temporary, never steady ones. My problem was I liked to party too much, never plan ahead, or was responsible.

Several letters later José told me that his mom had tracked down his birth certificate, and that he was in fact a year younger than he had believed. I joked that he was the only person I knew who was getting younger.

José's mom, whom he adored, was a Jehovah's Witness; José himself believed in God. He was keen to better himself, and took several study courses, including a Bible study.

I don't think I'm gifted at drawing, but thanks for the compliment. What I did was, to taught myself by watching other people, so I did the same when I was growing up trying to learn Inglish and Spanish. I speak both very fluent; not bad for someone who's education was very limited.

I began to have an inkling of the racial prejudice that both José and Tommy had faced in the USA. Both men had been careful to tell me early in our friendship about their colour and race, almost as though they were giving me a chance to withdraw if I wished. It was irrelevant to me, of course. Besides, I knew the statistics: if you are black or

Hispanic, you are much more likely to end up in prison than if you are white. This applies even more to the men on Death Row. Tommy had already lost one pen-friend, who stopped writing when she learned that he was black. "You're better off without her," I told him. He shrugged it off magnanimously: "It's no big deal if people feel that way about me."

I was angry that anyone would begin an association with a man in such a vulnerable position, and then abandon him for such a reason. We went on to have many discussions about racism, during which Tommy struggled to explain to me its origins, history and prevalence in his society. I failed to comprehend, insisting that there is no such thing as racial purity. "We're all a racial cocktail," I would insist, unable to understand how the colour of one's skin or place of origin could have any significance in personal relationships.

I found this contact with another culture fascinating and stimulating, and the letters lifted me from my own mundane English world into an entirely different place. If the men in prison were lonely and dependent on their correspondence, I was no less so: I was becoming more and more reliant on those messages from far away. The feeling of being needed was intoxicating, but not necessarily healthy. I loved receiving letters from both my prisoner friends, but I was especially close to Tommy. When his letters suddenly stopped for no apparent reason, I was devastated. I wondered if he had been executed without me knowing – after all, he was on Death Row and expected to die. If it happened, no one would be likely to inform me. My sense of loss was unbearable.

I knew there were plenty of reasons why letters might fail to arrive: public holidays in the USA or delays in the postal system in England; Tommy might have run out of stamps, or be segregated in "The Hole" for some misdemeanour, and deprived of writing materials. I knew all this, but I was quite unable to respond rationally to the sudden silence. My self-confidence was so fragile that the slightest problem knocked it flat; if I didn't get a reply when I expected one, I felt let down. I read into situations things that weren't there, and I was quick to feel rejected by everyone.

Even my children seemed to be a problem. My eldest daughter was being difficult, and I over-reacted to her typical teenage thoughtlessness. I wasn't even a very good mother, I thought. I felt useless, abandoned, panicky and nauseated. In fact I was in danger of descending into clinical depression – a place I had been to before. Several times in the past I had been thrown into that black pit by events around me – bereavements when my father and a close friend had died, troubles affecting other friends, or crises in my marriage. Sometimes I just wanted release from all my misery and frustration, and thoughts of death were almost inescapable.

Fortunately I came to my senses in time. I realized that I had become totally self-absorbed in my own miseries; my daughter was behaving entirely normally for her age; she didn't hate me. In any case, I couldn't go through with the idea of suicide. My fragile faith had never deserted me, though I confess I hung on to my belief as a kind of insurance policy, rather than because I could feel God at work in my life. I could never deny my experience of conversion (it was far too powerful), but it seemed a long way in the past, a sort of fading memory. I struggled to hold on.

> How long, O Lord, wilt thou quite forget me?
> How long wilt thou hide thy face from me?
> How long must I suffer anguish in my soul,
> Grief in my heart, day and night? (Psalm 13:1–2)

I was almost at the end of my tether when the longed-for letter arrived, and I tore it open, hoping for some explanation for the silence. I had invested so much significance in it, but the contents were an anti-climax. Tommy put the delay down to laziness on his part, and said he was sorry for any anxiety he had caused. "I would never do anything to cause you any kind of problems whatsoever, and please Penny, for my sake, never doubt our friendship because you are my soul-mate for life ... I still care about your well-being as my friend."

However, in another letter a few weeks later, he confessed the real reason behind the break in communications. Fearing that he was becoming too emotionally involved and dependent on me, he had decided to back off.

> The reason for the delay at the time is quite simple actually, although solutions to simple matters are not always so easy to find ... my feelings were beginning to take another direction beyond the normal pen-friend and I needed to stop the wheel for a moment to ask myself some very serious questions ... the very last thing a man in my situation needs to deal with is an emotional love interest because my future is so uncertain.

He knew all about loneliness.

> I've somewhat prepared myself for isolation from any kind of contact with the outside world, with the exception of my immediate family of course, at least until I'm able to confirm one way or the other is this the last button on Gabriel's coat for me ... in doing so, I live one day at a time.

He described with great clarity the battle going on in his head. "I kept looking at that first snap you sent me and all

I could think of was damn, she looks so peaceful and I wonder if she would mind sharing some of it with me." Attentive female, lonely male is an explosive combination. Several prisoners and their pen-friends had succumbed, but Tommy wasn't about to give in without a struggle. "I feel a cad ... I've done many bad things in my life, but stealing another man's wife isn't one of them."

I could sense the impatience creeping into his writing. In an effort to avoid the pain of separation he had made a Herculean effort to cut himself off mentally from the world beyond the prison gates. Now his relationship with me had forced him to reconsider.

It was a startling lesson to me: Tommy had shown more self-awareness than I had, and it had taken the loss of his letters to make me see how involved with him I had become. I realized that I needed to look closely at my side of this relationship, and the level of my dependence on Tommy. It was a sobering thought. I appreciated his integrity, but it made me realize that I had to show the same integrity in my own life, and face up to the very real problems in my marriage.

I began to tell him about my own personal difficulties, how unhappy I was, and how I had contemplated suicide when I was in the depths of depression. "I'm here to tell you that life is worth living," he wrote back. I felt ashamed. If he believed that, in his situation, how could I possibly give up on life?

> You are absolutely right in saying we are both prisoners with a different set of circumstances but we will draw strength from one another and continue to carry on as best we can through our communications ... I never question fate especially when the results turn out to be good and it sure was fate that brought us together, wouldn't you agree?

His generosity of spirit astounded me, and I felt mean beside him. To confide to someone on Death Row that you sometimes think of killing yourself is pretty self-indulgent. Tommy had no choice: the state would decide when his life ended. I was free to make my own choices, and I had been selfish enough to tell him my problems. I had offered him the lifeline of friendship, and followed it with yet another threat, that he might lose that too. I was sorry that I had inadvertently added another pressure to his intolerable situation, but I consoled myself that it must surely be better for him to know that he had someone fighting his corner and trying to give him moral and practical support.

Beside the new humility I felt, there was another feeling: a new awareness of how good my life actually was. It was so unexpected, that a man in such a dreadful, sterile situation could still enjoy life; that he could revel in each new morning as he walked across the compound, even though he had to eat disgusting meals, be locked in his prison cell, and remain under threat of a horrible end – yet he still thought it was good to be alive. It made my own problems pale into insignificance.

7

First Visit

MY FRIEND MARGARET had always taken an interest in my prison pen-friends – her husband also wrote to a man in Riverbend jail – but she never expected to be in contact herself. Then, in 1992, she made her annual visit to the Taizé community in France. There she met some Americans from Vanderbilt University, Nashville, who invited her to go and study there for part of her Master's degree. At first Margaret dismissed this idea as merely a light-hearted suggestion, made during a transient holiday friendship, so she was surprised and pleased when the same friends wrote and asked her when she was coming to the USA. She arranged her visit for later that year.

When I heard that she was planning a visit to the United States, I asked her to take over some goodies for Tommy, and post them there – it would be so much cheaper than airmail from England. She agreed, and wrote down the address. It was several weeks before I received a postcard from her. She hadn't posted my gifts for Tommy – she had taken them to the prison and handed them over in person! "I was able to meet Tommy, and he's very nice," she said.

I was astounded. I knew enough about prisons to know that you didn't just walk into them as if you were calling on a friend. The rules are very strict, and only those whose names appear on the approved visitor list are allowed to see inmates. However, Margaret's friends had been friendly and hospitable, and when they heard about her errand for me, they were determined to be as helpful as possible. One of them knew someone who was a friend of the governor's wife; they made a few telephone calls, and Margaret was allowed a visit.

When she returned to England she came to see me, and gave me a huge hug. "That's from Tommy," she said. "He asked me to pass it on to you. Anyway, you'll have to meet him for yourself – I promised him that I'd get you to come to the States with me soon. We'll visit him together."

I had never particularly wanted to visit America. It held no appeal for me, with its frenetic lifestyle, concrete jungles, consumerism and crime ... but now it held something else: one of my friends. To my surprise, I found myself agreeing to go.

Since I am a part-time lecturer, my holidays are restricted by academic terms. I had already made plans for the following year, but unexpectedly my booking for the October half-term holiday fell through, and my deposit was returned. October was a good time for Margaret, so everything was settled. The trip was on.

When I told Tommy of our plans, his response was typical.

In your letter you said you would try to get over here next October. Well my friend there is absolutely nothing in the world I would love more than to see you in person ... but Penny, I am not a selfish individual ... and I would not want you to travel thousands of miles for the sole purpose of visiting me ... we're talking about crossing an entire ocean and I am quite flattered indeed that you would come to the States just to see me yet I am thinking of the distance you must travel and of course the expense of it also.

I was concerned about where we would stay during our visit, but Tommy came up trumps. He sent me a copy of the prison magazine, which contained an advert for "Reconciliation", the Christian guest house. It served several prisons in the Nashville area, including Riverbend. I wrote to ask if they would be able to accommodate us, and the Reverend Katherine (known to her friends as Kaki) wrote back, welcoming us to stay with them. They were well used to people travelling long distances to Nashville, from Memphis, Knoxville and Chattanooga, as well as out of state from Georgia, Louisiana and beyond, but they had never had "foreigners" visiting from the other side of the Atlantic. She added: "I have met with Tommy on several occasions. He is one of my favourite people on the Unit. His gentle spirit and soft voice make him a wonderful person to visit. You have found a special person in Tommy."

Meanwhile, Tommy tried to prepare me for the reality of his life as a convicted murderer. He began with some experiences of his early days at the old prison, The Walls: "It was dog eat dog in those days. Only the toughest survived. In my time there, killings were commonplace. I personally saw three men murdered." He mentioned again how much he regretted his criminality and hoped that he might be given a chance to become a productive member of society, and enabled to give something back. I was still surprised that he had been convicted of a capital offence; though my knowledge of the US legal system was sketchy, I was sure that under English law he would have been charged with manslaughter. It was obvious that his lifestyle at the time and some previous minor convictions had counted against him. I was being initiated into the brutality of the American penal system, and I wondered how inmates such as Tommy learned to cope.

"How do you do it?" I asked in one letter.

"Simple," he replied. "I have no choice."

While we were planning for my visit, a new complication arose. I had answered a request by BBC Radio 4 for listeners with interesting hobbies, for a series called *Tuesday Lives*, which explored some of the unusual things ordinary people do. I wrote that I was a woman cricket reporter – and added, as an afterthought, that I also corresponded with prisoners. I admit that I was daydreaming that I might be "discovered" as a sports journalist and get the chance to spend the winters watching cricket in Australia! However, when they replied, they said that they were particularly interested in the prison angle, and my trip to meet Tommy.

I was delighted to have an opportunity to raise awareness of the issue of capital punishment, but I wasn't sure how Tommy would feel about it. He wasn't keen on publicity. I made it clear to the producers of the show that I would need to get Tommy's consent, and they agreed: the programme was scheduled to air in November, after my visit. They proposed a direct line to the jail so that we could talk live on the day, and they promised to contact the authorities to get permission for the radio link.

Then, suddenly, there was a change of schedule: the BBC wanted our contribution to be broadcast in June. The prison governor had agreed to the arrangements, but once again there was silence from Tommy; he didn't answer my urgent fax. I tried to contact the prison authorities myself, but they were curt and refused to let me talk to him; they said he wasn't interested. Then, on the very day of the broadcast, a letter arrived. Tommy said he was happy for me to take part, and to talk about our correspondence, but he would prefer not to be directly involved himself.

Let me try to explain this best I can on paper. After years of being subject to some of the most critical and negative publicity in print and my views taken out of context in the early stages of my sentence I guess I've just grown very thick-skinned in this area ... Americans are bloodthirsty and always have been but I didn't realize just how much until my first experience with the local media ... about four or five months after receiving this sentence. You wouldn't believe the feedback and the comments about me from total strangers. Some even suggested coming out to the prison and pulling the switch themselves if given the opportunity. It was such a bad experience I thought I should give another and try to clarify some of the issues concerning the death penalty, only this time I didn't catch a tidal wave of abusive comments, the paper did, for giving me a forum to express unpopular opinions in this part of the country.

I was glad that he went on to say that he had confidence in the BBC's integrity, and accepted my assurances that this was a reputable programme which would give him, via me, a fair hearing. "I won't try to tightrope on this issue but I'm deathly afraid of any type of interviews because of my personal past experience with the media."

He concluded that it was all right for the broadcast to take place, since it would not be heard in America. My opinion was that we should use whatever avenues were open to us to highlight the plight of men like Tommy, provided we were happy with the quality of the journalism. "You are your own best advertisement, Tommy," I wrote. "If people could only see the sort of man you are, they wouldn't contemplate pulling the switch on you."

Tuesday Lives went out on 22 June 1993, and all my friends thought it went well. We used an old tape of Tommy introducing some of his favourite songs on a cassette he'd sent me, plus a few short quotes from a letter, expressing his anticipation of my visit.

A few weeks later the BBC contacted me again, asking

if they might do a follow-up programme after Tommy and I had met. They arranged to telephone me while I was still in the USA, to record an interview and get my impressions of our long-awaited first meeting.

"Suppose you don't get on?" asked the BBC researcher. "We will," I replied confidently. I had been disappointed that Tommy felt unable to take part in the programme, but I knew I still had to prove to him that he could trust me. He insisted that he did:

> Will you please forgive me for the uncertainty I feel about any sort of publicity, good or bad ... I'm sure the people are on the up and up or you would not be involved in the first place ... I really cherish your letters and above all your sincere friendship and when I say we will be soul-mates for life Penny, you can take that to the bank. You may receive a sort of weird look from the window teller, but only because she doesn't know me!

The weeks slipped by. "You know I'm counting the days."

Margaret and I set off on our great adventure.

Our first view of the prison was from the imposing gateway, where we looked around and saw all those miles of razor wire. A few saplings had been planted on top of the grassy bank to the right, to form a screen in years to come. So this was a maximum security prison? It looked more like a modern factory or a sports centre – very different from the grim Victorian buildings I had visited in England.

We parked the car and went into the vestibule. Everything was immaculate: gleaming vinyl floor tiles; a few plastic chairs; a soft-drinks machine; a dollar-note changing machine; a bank of lockers; potted plants dotted around. Offices opened off a long corridor lined with photographs of the staff. It could have been the reception area of any commercial company. We waited nervously at a desk while a prison officer tapped in our details at his computer terminal, then he pushed a visitors' book towards us. We signed in, filling in our time of arrival, and our inmate's number and unit.

"We usually ask for your driver's licence, ma'am," said the officer, "but you English guys don't have photos on yours, do you?"

I handed over my old green driving licence, which the officers examined curiously, and my passport too. Both were returned to me with a locker key so that I could store my belongings securely. Then we were given a pass.

Armed with this document, we moved on to the next phase of the security system: a walk-through x-ray machine, an ultra-violet dye stamped on our hands, and a body search by a female guard, while our coats and small personal items were placed on a conveyor belt and screened again. Finally we were allowed to pass through a series of heavy, electrically operated gates and into the compound. We passed through another building where our hand-stamps were verified, and out to the housing units: several concrete buildings radiating out like the spokes of a wheel. The central area at the hub was surrounded by double rows of tall steel fencing, topped with yet more razor wire; from this four entrances opened onto the housing blocks.

We glanced around and spotted the word "Two" – our destination. Unit Two was Death Row, where men waited for years to learn their ultimate fate: a lifetime of imprisonment, or a nightmare extinction at the hands of the state. There was nothing to indicate that this block was any different from the others. We pressed a button beside the door, which opened slowly to admit us. I wondered why we needed to buzz for attention; I knew that our progress had been monitored every step of the way by the security cameras. Another guard took our passes and indicated the visiting room, where we could wait while Tommy was brought down.

The visiting room itself was surprisingly small. It was furnished with the bare minimum: several rows of plastic chairs, all linked together; two plastic dustbins; a microwave oven; and a shelf of battered books and toys. Three huge domed mirrors enabled the officer at the desk to see every part of the room. I don't remember how many people were waiting with us, for my mind was preoccupied. Would I recognize Tommy when he arrived? Margaret had seen him before, of course, but I had only seen those poor prison Polaroid photos.

Then the door opened and Tommy was rushing towards us, to hug first Margaret and then me, and I said, "Hello, Tommy. We made it at last!"

Throughout that first visit we chatted and laughed and held hands, just happy to have met at last. Tommy produced a bandanna with a Harley Davidson motif, and wiped his face and hands continuously. I teased him about it, knowing that while handkerchiefs were allowed, bandannas were not, and asked him why he was sweating in the cool, air-conditioned atmosphere. He admitted that he was very nervous, and we all laughed again.

The visit flew by, as did all the other visits we made in our two-week stay. Each time I entered the prison I was struck anew by the sterility of the environment. Everything and everyone in the place seemed to be regulated and controlled, so that the whole institution ran like clockwork, clean, efficient and cold. Men, visitors and staff alike were processed through the system, because only certainty and predictability could ensure security. There was no room for surprises here, and no humanity at all.

Alongside the communal area where we met with

Tommy stood a series of small booths; there, behind screens, sat the men who were not permitted the luxury of contact with friends and family. How hard it must be to try to communicate in such a situation. How hard to explain to a child that he cannot cuddle his father; how hard for a wife or a mother, unable even to hold hands for comfort. The rest of us take such gestures so much for granted.

In those six visits I got to know Tommy even better than before. There is a profound difference between reading someone's words on a page and talking with him face to face. I'm not sure exactly what sort of person I was expecting: a tough, street-wise guy, smooth-talking and self-centred, perhaps – after all, he was a murderer. His letters hadn't been quite like that, but how much of my own interpretation had I put into my reading of them? What I found was a quiet man, thoughtful, cautious and sensitive. I had no doubt that he could take care of himself if need be, but with us he was softly spoken, dignified, gracious, polite, and interested in others. He had sophisticated tastes, enjoying visits to art galleries, long country walks, wearing cashmere and eating sushi. It wasn't the cultural background I had expected of a man on the row. He looked and sounded so out of place in that maximum security prison that I had a strong sense of the surreal. How on earth could he remain sane in such a hostile environment?

Tommy had promised to tell me more about his life and his crime, and on the second visit he did so, though I could sense his embarrassment. He didn't glory in his past behaviour and lifestyle, and it was obvious that he had tried hard to put it behind him. His candour was disarming: he didn't try to make excuses or to blame anyone else. "It's all down to me. This is where the buck stops," he insisted.

I thought how much he had achieved during his years behind bars. He had come to terms with the person he was, and developed into a well-adjusted adult. He was truly whole. Many of us who carry much lighter burdens of guilt never get to that stage because we are not big enough to admit our faults and failings, so we cannot move forward. Tommy was a big man in more ways than one. I was amazed that he didn't show resentment towards the people who had put him in jail. His legal representation at his trial had been inadequate, and it was an all-white jury which had convicted him of capital murder. With a more experienced and effective lawyer and a jury of his peers his defence might have been accepted, and he would have been sentenced for manslaughter, a lesser charge. Tommy had always insisted that he had acted in self-defence, and I had always thought, "Well, you would say that, wouldn't you?" Now, however, I had the opportunity to speak to several other people about his case, including some with legal training. They agreed that Tommy had been very unlucky at his trial.

What is to be done in such a situation? Where is there justice in our imperfect world? Some words from Psalm 130 came into my head:

Out of the depths have I called to thee, O Lord;
Lord, hear my cry.
Let thy ears be attentive
To my plea for mercy.
If thou, Lord, shouldest keep account of sins,
Who, O Lord, could hold up his head?
But in thee is forgiveness,
And therefore thou art revered.
I wait for the Lord with all my soul ...
For in the Lord is love unfailing,
And great is his power to set men free. (Psalm 130: 1–5, 7)

Something very profound and shocking had happened during those two weeks in Nashville. All my preconceptions about the sort of men who end up on Death Row were shattered. I had begun to know Tommy through his letters, but meeting him face to face made all the difference. I was surprised to realize how likeable he was, how ordinary, how good a friend. Of course, I didn't meet all the men who were locked up with him in Unit Two – I never encountered the men who really were dangerous or mentally ill. But I met and got to know enough of the others to realize that most of my preconceived ideas were wrong. These were not monsters of evil, or criminals who needed to be taught the error of their ways. Most of them were clear-sighted enough to know where they had gone wrong; they knew exactly what their criminal behaviour had been, and most of them regretted it. They did not need to be brutalized.

I am a passionate gardener, and as I walked the interminable corridors and compounds on my way to the visiting room in Unit Two, I often wondered how long it had been since any of these men had smelt the perfume of a rose. Was it really necessary to keep them in such a sterile environment? Was there no better way of dealing with them? It was incredible to think of someone being kept in prison for twenty years. I had expected to see walking hulks, the dried-out shells of men. Yet they had somehow retained their imagination, their warmth, and their interest in the outside world. They were tremendously alive.

Prison visits took up only two hours of the day, and I was only allowed six visits, so I had plenty of spare time. I spent much of it helping out at Reconciliation with housework, secretarial work and any other chores that needed doing. It was a busy organization: its volunteers held midweek meetings for prisoners' families, and ran parties for their children; they lobbied local businesses for funding; they represented inmates at parole hearings, and attended mediation panels. I got on well with the other volunteers and made some wonderful friendships. Some of the prisoners and their families thought it was rather odd that a middle-aged lecturer from England should want to travel halfway round the world to visit people who were rejected by their own society, but they, too, accepted me.

I found that I was busy and fulfilled in a way that I never felt when I was at home in England, and I returned home with many questions in my heart. I wondered if I was being called to move to Nashville and make my home there, among my new friends. When I voiced this thought to Tommy in a letter, his response was typically pragmatic: "Your place is home with your kids."

I knew he was right, but I so often wished I was closer to him. One day he wrote to me at length about his childhood in Chattanooga, and the pain he still felt over his parents' death, and I felt frustrated at not being there to talk to him, to share his pain, and to try to bring him some comfort. I was touched by his willingness to open his heart and admit to his own desolation; he said that he felt like screaming at the top of his voice to God, for allowing such a cruel thing to happen. I wrote back immediately.

> I realize that yet another door has been opened between us. Such total candour and trust is a new experience for me, so I must catch my breath a little, but I do thank you for sharing these thoughts with me ... I have no easy answers. Indeed, I have no answers at all. Life often seems perverse and cruel to me, and I have moments of hating God with such a fierce hatred that I frighten myself with my own depth of passion ... As I write these inadequate words, my own eyes have welled up with tears. You were lucky to have these people in your life, Tommy, and they you.

It occurs to me that Jesus must have had much the same anger as you when he was hanging on the cross, an innocent victim of prejudice and political expediency, and God must have wept for his only son's pain ... Indeed, it must have been worse for him, the creator and maintainer of the universe, for he had the power to *stop* it all, to turn the tables and reverse the action, but did not, because Jesus' death *had* to be, in order to bring about the life of others ...

All life is precious and God-given. Some people corrupt their lives and drift so far away from what they might have been that it's difficult to see anything positive in them. They may seem less worth while, therefore, than others, and easier to justify when snuffed out. This is the precise same attitude that executing states have of their men on the Row, and needless to say, is not one I share. Make no mistake on this one, I believe in the power of evil just as strongly ... I will tell you now quite plainly, that when I met you, I was taken completely by surprise by the goodness I perceived in you. Beneath it all, you were on the right side, Tommy ... we must all make a conscious decision each day, as to which side of the line we will walk ... your own free will, will always tend to do what is right, unerringly. You are good at heart.

Like I say, I have no answers. If I did, I would not be as troubled as I often am. The "peace which passeth all understanding" is so elusive, so desirable ... We are all islands ... Living is a lonely, frightening occupation. All we can hope is that we will discover another nearby island in our sea of troubles, I guess.

Having written those words, I was left wondering if I had ever been a Christian in any meaningful sense of the word. I never had a problem accepting that our Lord Jesus had risen from the dead, but as for the rest of us, that was something I found harder. It seemed to me that this life was all there was, and we must do our best here and now. To expect rewards in another life was foolish and unreasonable. We should enjoy what personal happiness we could, provided it was not at the expense of another. Jesus sent his Spirit to help us in our struggles here on earth, but my theology stopped at that point: the idea of an afterlife threw up too many questions. One of the central tenets of my faith always eluded me, leaving me bereft of that hope. My journey of faith was still right at the beginning.

8

Divorce

WHILE MY CONTACTS WITH PRISONERS were becoming more and more important to me, my home life became increasingly strained. I was fighting to keep my marriage alive, and I didn't want to admit defeat. I had a horror of becoming one more to add to the divorce statistics.

When we read in the popular press about celebrity marriages being dissolved after a matter of months or even weeks, we may have our suspicions about the degree of seriousness with which they were entered into in the first place. We feel that the parties involved were making their vows with an unspoken proviso: "Yes, I agree to all this today, but if something happens tomorrow to make me feel differently, it's no big deal. I'll just get out. I'm certainly not prepared to stay in a relationship which doesn't measure up to my expectations."

That wasn't the way I approached my own wedding. I had intended my vows to be for life, and though I had found my marriage a disappointment, I had persevered and tried to do my best within it. They say that girls often marry men who are like their fathers, and I guess that was true of my choice of Ian: like Dad, he was loyal and dependable, and never demonstrative or effusive. I was an organized person, always prepared for all contingencies: I bought my Christmas presents in the new year sales; I planned my college lessons with meticulous care; I never forgot a birthday; I even planned the births of my children for the closed season, when there were no cricket matches! I liked everything in my life to be tightly controlled, because that way I had power over it and felt safe. Yet I couldn't control my own emotions. At first I had welcomed the security of my solid, reliable husband – now I found him tedious and boring.

Over the years we had drifted apart, in spite of all my efforts. For a whole ten-year period, from 1983 to 1993, we had no physical relationship at all. Sexual coldness reinforced my feelings of rejection, and led to further coldness. As time went on it became more and more impossible to break out of the vicious circle. I felt unloved, unloving and unlovable. Nevertheless I was still trying to keep up appearances with friends, neighbours, colleagues and our church congregation. Over the years I had become a good actor, hiding my real feelings from the world, and preserving the façade of a happy family life. I was used to escaping from awkward situations by making a joke and laughing things off, but underneath I felt hollow.

At last even I began to see the hypocrisy of all this. A couple of church services in particular spoke to my heart and made me realize that my desperate clinging on to respectability was in fact a way of living a lie. One of them was led by Dick, a retired vicar and a new member of our congregation. His text was Matthew 5, the Beatitudes, and his theme was "the kingdom of God". He began by describing his earlier life as a GP in a wealthy Norfolk practice, with his large house and garden, his swimming pool, and his comfortable lifestyle. Even when he was ordained and took on a more modest role as a hospital chaplain, he said, he still felt that he had a certain standing in the community. It was only after he retired and moved north that he realized that the kingdom had nothing to do with wealth or position. As a pensioner, he felt that he had been stripped of his social status: when asked his profession he could no longer claim to be a doctor, a higher-rate tax payer, or even a vicar. Now he was just himself, with no rank or position to hide behind. He had been taught a lesson in humility: never judge people by their job, or lack of one, nor by their bank balance.

Most sermons are quickly forgotten, but Dick's talk stayed with me. It somehow tied in with the way I related to people in prison: they had been deprived of all wealth, power and social position. I had always hated pretension, and these were people with none – no flashy car, no designer wardrobe, no nice house, no impressive career. When they were all dressed the same, depersonalized in prison uniform, all that was left was the real human being inside. Raw humanity and a strange sort of honesty shone out, and I found it attractive. I began to think about the nature of reality and the role of honesty in relationships.

The second church service also spoke to me directly. Its theme was reality, and it started with a short sketch acted by members of the congregation. In it, two women were discussing a third person, who had conducted a blazing argument with his wife in church. One woman disapproved; the other said that if the church was a family, then you should be able to be yourself within it, and expect support, not judgement. The punch line, of course, was "Well, it still wasn't a very good example for the vicar to set!" It made us all laugh, but it set me thinking. Was I really so terrified of the reactions of my church family that I kept up a pretence about my own life?

The sketch was followed by a retelling of the story of the Velveteen Rabbit. In it, the smart, plush toy rabbit learns how to become "real" – by being loved by his child owner. It is a painful process, and over the years he becomes battered and worn, but he is rewarded by the knowledge that to the child he is much more than a toy –

he is real. The children in the service loved the story, but it spoke to me too.

I had already come to the conclusion that the reason I got on so well with prisoners was that they were "real" people, "up-front" with all their faults and shortcomings. I hated affectation. I often wished that when someone said, "How are you?" that it was acceptable to reply, "Well, actually, things aren't so good at the moment." Why were people so scared to show their true feelings? Why were they so concerned about other people's reactions? I particularly liked the old saying, "Before my twenties, I didn't care what people thought of me. In my thirties, I worried all the time what they thought of me. And in my fifties, I knew they hardly thought about me at all!" Didn't that put things into perspective?

That was when I realized that I, who sought reality and truthfulness in others, was actually guilty of the greatest hypocrisy of all. I was living a lie by pretending that my marriage was a real one. The only honest course of action was to get a divorce.

Nevertheless, I found it incredibly hard to take that step. For a start, I came from the sort of background where marriage breakdown was regarded with shame, and where it still carried a stigma. In addition, I felt sure that God did not approve of divorce. Marriage was for life, come what may. I felt a failure, and my personal pride was battered by the realization that I had been unable to make a success of the most important relationship in my life. Where was God in all this? I had Christian friends whose marriages had foundered because they had married unbelieving partners, yet Ian and I weren't in that situation. We shared the same beliefs – so why hadn't we been able to work things out? We had the help of the Holy Spirit in our lives – so how could this have happened to us? I was filled with confusion and sadness.

The other difficulty for me was my total lack of self-confidence. I was afraid of taking such a huge step: I didn't feel able to do anything to lift myself out of my miserable state. This was where my friendship with Tommy came to my rescue. Knowing that he valued me as a friend had already begun to improve my sense of self-worth. Little things helped: one day he said to me, "Have you never thought of wearing earrings? I notice that you make jewellery but you don't wear it much." It was a small comment, but it was significant of something much deeper: I had lost so much self-esteem that I no longer thought of myself as attractive in any way, so I didn't bother about my appearance. I hadn't entirely "let myself go", as they say – I always dressed tidily and smartly – but there didn't seem to be any point in personal adornment. Now I went and dug out some earrings and started wearing them.

Tommy and the others were always asking for photographs, and I sent them, even though I hated having my picture taken. He asked about the whole family, wanted to know what my daughters were doing, and took an interest in everything I told him. He was living his life partly through us, which was understandable, yet this level of interest was intoxicating for me. I had always felt undervalued, and to have letters from the US saying, in effect, "I'm pleased to have you in my life" made me walk a little taller. I was important to someone!

When I went through a period of real depression, Tommy wasn't just concerned, he set about trying to build a support network for me. He put me in touch with people on the outside whom he trusted, such as his sister and brother, and a friend called Paul who was a church minister in Maine. Tommy was a good listener, and he was acting as a counsellor, in a very down-to-earth way. He didn't treat me as a hysterical female who was just going through a bad patch: he took me seriously. At the same time, his comments were challenging. He made me see that I wasn't powerless to change my situation; I was only a victim of my own inertia. If I was unhappy, I had to take control of the situation and make something happen.

Gradually I began to see more clearly. Tommy was on Death Row, totally at the mercy of other people; I, on the other hand, was not in a prison, other than one I had made for myself. I did have power over my own life, but I had allowed it to ebb away until I felt helpless. I needed someone to activate me, and Tommy's letters helped me to formulate a way out. I realized that I *could* act to change my situation. I applied for a divorce.

I knew the girls would be upset, but the person I feared telling most of all was my elderly mother. I was sure she would be mortified. However, her reaction wasn't as bad as I had expected. When I told her that I had been unhappy for most of our married life, she said that she had suspected as much. I was relieved, but I wished she had said something earlier: it would have made such a difference if I had been able to share my feelings with someone. She came from a generation which did not pry into other people's lives, but I wished that we had been closer.

Getting the divorce was straightforward. I decided to do it all myself, for two reasons: cost and friendship. Ian had always said that he thought that having lawyers involved in a relationship breakdown set the parties at one another's throats, and I didn't want any ill-feeling or bitterness. It was bad enough to be severing a union of twenty-two years; I wanted to salvage some kind of friendship and positive feelings. We sat down and listed all our joint possessions, and came to an amicable agreement about who should have what. I presented our plans to the court, and as the children were almost adults, the question of access didn't arise. Three months later, I had my decree nisi.

Though the legal side of the divorce was relatively

painless, the emotional side was anything but. I found it difficult to come to terms with the notion of being divorced. To me, marriage was not primarily a legal arrangement, so being issued with the relevant document didn't make me feel free: in my mind, I was still bound. Marriage to me was a sacrament, a spiritual mystery far more binding than any licence, and there was no help available from the church for finding release from those spiritual ties. I was going through a mental struggle, and in addition, I was very lonely. However, this was nothing new – it is possible to be just as lonely in a relationship as when one is single. Now I had to face the future alone, and the only thing I could hold on to was the thought that I still had God in my life. He had a plan for me, even though I couldn't see what it was. And, of course, I had my friends. I would be all right.

9

Travels in America

I N MARCH 1994 I MADE MY SECOND TRIP to the USA, this time travelling alone. The prospect was quite daunting: I was sure I wouldn't be able to find my way around unaided. I'm notorious for having no sense of direction, and it was a family joke that I was capable of getting lost in my home town. Then there were so many things to organize: insurance, flights, currency, car hire and accommodation. On holiday I had always relied on my husband to sort out things like that, and on my previous trip to the USA I had travelled with Margaret and benefited from her experience. This time I was on my own.

In fact I surprised myself: my arrangements went off without a hitch. My travel expenses had been partly paid by a generous award from the Diocese of Lichfield, so I didn't have to worry about money as much as usual, and I had friends at Reconciliation who were looking forward to my visit and who would help me when I arrived. All the same, I was relieved when I managed to get myself and my luggage safely to the guest house, and presented myself next day at the prison. I was looking forward to seeing Tommy, and also renewing my friendships with the people on the outside.

One of my contacts was Paul, Tommy's minister friend. He had studied in Nashville, and he too supported the campaign against the death penalty. He had written to me before my visit:

I understand when you say that Tommy seems out of place in prison. I have that feeling, even though I've never seen him anywhere else. I know that he seems more out of place there than he would in my living room ... It is clear to me that he has deep commitments among his family and friends that he has put on hold, and I know this troubles him deeply. His warm humour and his sharp interest in the world around him are his appealing traits.

That feeling was reinforced when I visited Tommy this time: it was so good to see him again, and yet painful to realize that although my own life had moved on, he was still stuck in the same no-man's-land between life and death. It struck me yet again how cruel it was to make people live for such extended periods with the threat of execution hanging over them. Every day of life was a bonus, yet there was an extra dimension to imprisonment on Death Row that made it a worse punishment than serving a life sentence on an ordinary wing. The awareness of the execution chamber was always at the back of my mind.

The prisoners themselves had devised methods of coping with this knowledge, and they lived their lives within the system as best they could. For instance, they always had little scams on the go. There was a gambling syndicate, with one inmate keeping a "book" on the football results, and the men wagering a book of stamps or some cigarettes on the outcome. Then there were the men who worked in the data plant, who had discovered an ingenious way to make a little extra cash. They were paid piece-work, so the more key-strokes they registered, the more money they made. They found a way of tapping the keys randomly in between pieces of work, adding to their daily totals. John, the civilian in charge, never reported them. Instead, he let them know that he was on to them, and that if they carried on with their tactics, he would be deducting a large percentage of their pay cheque. The men put a stop to that one themselves. It was partly that they valued their jobs (there was always a waiting list for the chance to work in data) but also because they genuinely liked John. He treated them fairly and spoke to them like equals; at Christmas he used to bring in home-cooked treats for them – a welcome change from the bland prison stodge.

On one of my visits I got to know Walt, who sometimes cleaned the unit and helped out in the kitchens. He told me about another illicit prison activity. One day a friendly guard had offered me a coffee, but when I asked for sugar, there was none to be had. It seemed that a lot of sugar had gone missing from the kitchens, and the authorities had discovered that the men were stealing it to brew hooch. Their secret was exposed when there were several minor explosions in the cell block when some of the fermenting liquor got a bit too frisky! Walt lost his job, as well as his A level status.

Making that first visit alone was a ground-breaking experience for me. If I had lost confidence during my marriage, I had lost even more during the divorce. I had been apprehensive about making arrangements and dealing with everything from bureaucracy to car rentals. Now I was delighted: I had proved that I could look after myself, and the sense of achievement was exhilarating. Now I knew I could manage alone, and I knew that I would return. My prison correspondence was a very important part of my life, but I also knew how important it was for Tommy to know that I regarded him as a real friend, not just a hobby. Friends like to meet, and as he couldn't visit me, I would go to him. Somehow I would find the money for my travelling expenses.

I took a second part-time job to finance my travels,

working as an attendant at a local garage, getting up at five a.m. or taking the bank holiday shifts to fit around my college commitments. The work was hard and the pay was poor, but it helped and I was glad of it. With each successive trip to the USA I gained in confidence, and I was gathering around me an ever-widening circle of friends and acquaintances, both inside and outside jail. I took Hilary and Alison with me several times – I was anxious to involve them as I had when visiting English jails, and anyway I preferred to travel with a companion. They enjoyed the trips and quickly established friendships of their own.

Often we would stay at the Reconciliation guest house, but sometimes we spent part of the time in Chattanooga, Murfreesborough or Franklin, where we had other friends. Invariably their first response on meeting us was, "We *love* your accent!" Our reply was, "We don't have an accent. *You're* the ones with the accent!"

These good friends were always very concerned for our safety, so far from home, and in an alien culture. They deluged us with helpful advice: don't be too friendly, we were warned. Never stop to ask the way (something I had to do about three times a day, on average). Always lock your car door when you get in. Never offer anyone a lift. According to them, we were prey to every criminal in town, and I tried to keep calm and preserve a sense of proportion about the dangers lying in wait for us in the big city. Still, I must admit that we did have several exciting moments.

One such incident happened one afternoon when I had gone to mail some letters for Reconciliation. I was walking back to the office – not a recommended pursuit, as pedestrians are definitely an endangered species on American streets. It was a poor part of town, and the street was lined with the pawn shops and thrift stores that cater for the less affluent members of society. On the left was a grassy area and a telephone kiosk, and inside it a smartly dressed black man was picking through the contents of a wallet. When he saw me passing, he came out and called, "Hey, ma'am!"

I spun round and greeted him cheerfully.

"I just found this," he said, holding out the wallet. "Someone must have left it in here. What d'you think I should do?"

I suggested looking inside for the owner's name and address, or perhaps taking it down to the police station.

"Naw, we don't need to do that," he said. "Let's you and me split it and no one will be any the wiser." He flicked through a fat bundle of dollar bills, and produced a clear plastic bag containing what looked like uncut diamonds, which he pushed under my nose, temptingly.

"This could be our lucky day!" he exclaimed. "Don't you want to be rich?" Of course, naïve as I am, even I had smelt a rat by now. The man indicated a car parked beside the phone kiosk. "Come and sit in my car and we'll count this lot out."

"No thanks," I said, hurrying away, "I'd rather be poor." My friends told me later that this was a common ploy, and that I was lucky the guy hadn't pulled a gun on me.

On another occasion my friend Maria had flown from California to meet me in Nashville. We had planned a two-day vacation together, sight-seeing in Music City. On the first day we went downtown in daylight, mooched around the shops and went for a meal in a restaurant. When we emerged, darkness had fallen, and we were in trouble: we couldn't remember where we had left the hire car. Maria had health problems and was only able to walk short distances, but we toured the streets, slowly and painfully, for more than an hour.

Eventually, thoroughly lost and disoriented, we saw a police car parked by the side of the road, so I went up and tapped on the window. (This is also not something to be recommended in America.) The gorgeous black cop inside gave me a distrustful look and slowly lowered the window. "Yeah?" he enquired.

I explained our problem, and he was obviously reassured by my English accent.

"You two ladies don't want to be wandering around this part of town at night. Hop in."

He patiently drove us round and round until we spotted our hire car, standing abandoned in an otherwise empty street. Thanking him, we tried to get out of the car, only to find that we couldn't: there are no handles on the back doors of police cars! We had to wait for him to set us free, and see us safely on our way home. Once back in our car and on the road, we joked about our conversation with the helpful policeman. He had asked us politely what we were doing in Nashville, and we had replied vaguely that we were visiting friends. We wondered if we would have had such courteous treatment if he had known that our friends were on Death Row. We later discovered that we had been picked up right outside the local hostel for the city's drug addicts, alcoholics and down-and-outs.

It wasn't just these minor cultural confusions that beset me: the weather in the United States is altogether more dramatic than the gentle conditions we are used to in England. For a start, there are the tornadoes.

One Easter Hilary and I were spending a few days staying with friends in Chattanooga. We saw all the usual tourist attractions: the Chattanooga Choo-Choo, the new aquarium and all four shopping malls. On Good Friday we drove the two hundred miles or so to Nashville, visited Tommy, and stayed at the Reconciliation guest house over the weekend. On the following Tuesday, driving back again, we had the car radio tuned to our favourite station, the Soft Rock channel. We were surprised to hear breaks in the transmission for announcements by the emergency services. The Governor had declared Chattanooga a disaster area, and the Red Cross had set up posts in the shopping malls for the distribution of emergency aid. Even then, it didn't really register that we were heading into trouble. There wasn't much sign of it, either, until we turned off into the new housing estate where our friends lived.

I may have no sense of direction, but Hilary has, and so she navigates while I drive. This time, though, she was bewildered. We drove the entire length of the street without seeing any landmark we recognized. There should have been a large house on the corner by our turning, but it had disappeared. We eventually stumbled on the right street and hurried to find our friends.

The tornado, the first in living memory to hit Chattanooga, had struck just hours after we had driven away westwards on Good Friday. Most of the homes along the road into the housing development had gone, reduced to piles of matchwood. At the side of the road, groups of people were still standing around, dazed and staring in disbelief. Some houses were untouched; others had gaping holes in their roofs, or had the upper storeys sliced off, leaving the ground floor intact. Our friends and their children had spent the night crouched in a cupboard for shelter, with only a torch for light. They had been lucky: their house was still standing, with only a little damage to a rear door, which no longer closed – though they were still concerned, because they knew this could be a symptom of more serious structural problems. Their neighbours hadn't fared so well. One house had blown away entirely, and a family of five had survived by sheltering in the bathtub.

No one was killed in that night of terror, but millions of dollars' worth of damage was done. The families in the poor part of town were the worst off: most of them lived in trailers, which offered no resistance to the tornado, and most of them were unable to afford insurance. It was a sobering sight to see so many families left with nothing but the clothes they stood up in. I had taken a few snapshots of the place when we arrived; now I took another set, a "before and after" reminder of the power of nature. It was a humbling experience. "Israel, prepare to meet your God. It is he who forges the thunder and creates the wind, who showers abundant rain on the earth" (Amos 4:12–13).

On another visit one February, we were stranded on the tarmac at Chicago airport by a blizzard. It was what the Americans called a "total whiteout", and we had visions of spending the entire winter trapped in Chicago, waiting for the thaw to set in. However, the inhabitants of the windy city treated our drama as absolutely routine. They came out and sprayed the plane all over with antifreeze; then they sprayed it again, till it was bright blue all over. Twenty minutes later, we took off. Hilary adores flying and could answer questions on Mastermind with aircraft as her specialist subject, so she was entertaining me throughout the wait with explanations of exactly how and why we would crash if the wings and engines froze over. The man beside her looked decidedly unhappy and kept crossing himself nervously.

We had other alarms that were mostly caused by my own blunders, and these almost always seemed to involve hire cars. For some reason, the cars I hired were always inconspicuous, and I was for ever losing them on the vast expanses of car parking lots. I spent hours walking up and down searching for them. I was delighted on one trip to be offered a bright purple car, which I immediately christened Bill Berry – I knew he would stand out in a crowd and I'd be able to find him easily!

Considering my exemplary thirty-eight-year driving

record in the UK, I seem to have a remarkable number of problems once I am driving in the USA. On one visit I arrived at the prison in the early morning, while it was still dark. I absent-mindedly left the headlights on, and returned to find that the battery was quite flat. Now if you sit around on a car parking lot outside a maximum security facility for more than a couple of minutes, the guards don't like it. They think you're planning to spring someone, so they drive up to you, showing just a hint of rifle barrel. I found it disconcerting.

Eventually, of course, they realized that I wasn't a great security threat, and after examining the car for signs of life (there were none: when I kill a car, I kill it dead) they allowed me to call the rental company. They, in turn, were very surprised when I told them where to deliver the replacement vehicle – yes, they heard right the first time. I was indeed parked on the front lot of a maximum security prison.

On another occasion I noticed that the drive from Murfreesborough to Nashville was taking longer than usual. The car wasn't pulling very well, but I wasn't worried until I smelled burning rubber. That was when I realized that we had driven thirty miles down the inter-state with the handbrake on. Our friends in the prison told us to be sure to check the brakes before setting off for home, so I drove once round the prison grounds pumping my foot on the pedal, with the car lurching like a kangaroo. The guards watched our progress with amusement – I could just imagine the jokes about women drivers!

One of my more memorable experiences was with a company which went by the encouraging name of "Rentawreck". The two guys who ran the business were straight out of *The Dukes of Hazzard*. The insisted on calling me "Missy Penny" (which made me feel like Miss Ellie in *Dallas*), and assured me that their cars weren't really wrecks – it was just that they were older vehicles, and cheaper too, since the firm's location outside the airport meant they didn't have to pay airport fees.

They supplied me with a great gas-guzzling brute of a car, and a telephone number in case of trouble. Alarm bells were already ringing: my careful budgeting would be ruined if I had to keep filling up with petrol. I needn't have worried. That car wasn't going anywhere. It broke down outside the guest house and refused to move. In the end I had to call my hillbilly friends and get them to supply a replacement, which they did with admirable promptness and good humour. They were adamant that no one had ever had such a problem with one of their cars, and I believed them. They were so kind and willing to help, that I recommended them to my dear friends Mary and Jean, who were also visiting prisoners in the same state. I hoped they enjoyed meeting the Rentawreck staff as much I had.

Whenever we were in the USA we enjoyed meeting up with our considerable band of friends. How well God was looking after us, both keeping us safe in our travels and providing us with social and emotional support. All these people were hospitable, generous and like-minded in their active opposition to state killing. So few people in America share those views that those who do tend to know each other, and club together for mutual support. Several of the anti-death-penalty groups seemed to hold their meetings over lunch at cheap eating houses, so we soon sampled the gastronomic delights of all the Wendy's, Mcdonalds and Taco Bells within a twenty-mile radius of the jails.

My friend Harmon (whom I had met at meetings of the Campaign Against State Killing) was devoted to the cause. Whenever I was in Tennessee we would meet to catch up with all the gossip and news of the men's legal status in the light of various court rulings. We always met up at the same downtown restaurant, where they served Harmon's favourite lemon meringue pie. Reverend Joe was also a staunch campaigner and writer against the death penalty, and he was pastor to many of the guys at Riverbend; his tastes were less predictable. He liked to show me a new eating place at every trip. Some were wonderful: a Jewish deli where they did a great line in bagels with cream cheese, a restaurant specializing in southern fried chicken, or a really good burger bar. Others were not quite so much to our taste. Joe was convinced that the "Brits" had very conservative palates, and he thought it was his mission in life to educate us. Thus it was that we ended up in "Bros", a Cajun restaurant for truckers.

Joe's in-laws came from Louisiana, so the whole family was used to eating the spicy Cajun food. Hilary and I were not. We sat there, the only two females in the place, sur-rounded by loud, burly drivers, gingerly sipping bowls of the hottest gumbo imaginable. The waitress must have seen our expressions. When we left she said, "Have a nice day, ladies. I guess we may not be seeing you again, huh?"

At our next meeting, Joe said he had another place to take us.

"No more fire-water, Joe! Promise?" I pleaded.

"OK. I know you English guys have delicate digestions and can't cope with anything that's not totally insipid," he replied. I should have been warned when I heard that the place was called "Sweats". To emphasize his utter con-tempt for our refined English tastebuds, Joe ordered the hottest dish on the menu and sprinkled it liberally with fiery sauce, which I told him I would happily use as paint-stripper.

There was no doubt that in spite of our shared lan-guage, sometimes we felt very far from home. This was especially true at Christmas. At the time of year when everyone on the outside is getting ready to celebrate the festivities with their loved ones, the men on Death Row are painfully aware that their own families have an empty seat at the table. The end of the year is a reminder that another twelve months have passed. They are at least still alive, but it's a poor kind of living, spending every day contemplating a violent end to your life; unable to move around at will, shower or use the phone without permission; watching your back in case a fellow prisoner takes a dislike to you; looking forward to a visit, only to be told that the prison is on lock-down and all visits are cancelled.

I was surprised to see how few men had visits over the holiday period. Then I learned the reason: the prison staff cut the visiting hours by half, so it was hardly worth while for families to make a long journey just for a couple of hours. If they got held up in traffic, their journey would be wasted, and they'd have to turn round and go home without even setting foot inside the prison.

I visited Tommy twice at Christmas time: once in 1995, and again in 1997. He always tried to make sure I enjoyed our visits, and whatever his inner feelings he was up-beat, smiling and attentive. Once or twice, however, I caught a far-off look in his eye, as if his thoughts were elsewhere. Then in an instant he was back, bright and funny, the Tommy I knew and loved.

We found things to laugh about, even at this most sensitive time. The prison authorities put an artificial Christmas tree in the visiting room, decorated with tinsel and coloured baubles. It looked incongruous in that bare room, and there seemed to be very few visitors to admire it. Yet some must have come, because over the period of two or three weeks I noticed something: at every visit the tree was a little less bright. Slowly all the decorations were disappearing, and the tree was being stripped bare. The guys were sneaking them off and giving them to their mums, sisters and girlfriends, the only gifts they had to give.

Bob, who ran the Reconciliation guest house, did his utmost to celebrate the season. He put up a tree in the foyer, sang carols at the top of his tuneless voice, and cooked a delicious turkey for us all to share, complete with winter greens and sweet potatoes. His office door was decorated with cards from all the many visitors who appreciated having this cheap, safe and welcoming place to stay, just a short bus ride from all the Nashville prisons. He even bought and wrapped a small gift for each of us.

It was all a new experience for me, and I was horrified by my reaction. I hated it all. I hated being away from home at Christmas; I hated sweet potatoes; I hated the fact that in America, Christmas Day is like any other day – people go out to see a movie after lunch. Boxing Day is unknown, and shops scarcely have time to shut their doors before they are open for business again. I had never been more aware of my own Englishness. I missed all the traditions from home – the crackers, carols from King's, old films on TV, the midnight service, children's nativity plays, chipolatas, mince pies, the Queen's speech. Most of all, I missed the strange, intangible peace and stillness that descends after all the last-minute rush to get every-thing bought, wrapped or cooked.

I was astonished at myself. Wasn't I the one who had always deplored what had happened to Christmas? I had always claimed to dislike the over-indulgence, the com-mercialism and the general disregard for its true mean-ing. Now I realized how many of those things had become part of the fun of Christmas at home, and I missed them. Despite the tree in the hall, the turkey and Bob's enthusi-astic carolling, Christmas Day was bleak, and passed almost unnoticed. My mood was low, and made lower by the increased tension in the prison. I vowed never to return again at this time of year.

It was only as I prayed and reflected on the true meaning of Christmas that I recognized my selfish disappointment and simple homesickness for what it was. I was focusing on myself and my own wants, not on what God wanted me to do. What could be closer to the spirit of the day than to share it with the outcasts, the poor and the unloved? However uncomfortable and unappealing my day had been, I was where God wanted me to be. "When I was hungry, you gave me food; when thirsty, you gave me drink; when I was a stranger, you took me into your home, when naked you clothed me; when I was ill, you came to my help; when in prison you visited me" (Matthew 25:35–36).

Two years later, I approached the visit in a different frame of mind. I decided to attend a church service, to get into the spirit of things, so I went along with Reverend Joe. His church was called Christ Church (the same as my church at home), and his daughter was making her debut with the choir. Soon I was caught up in the familiar readings and carols, telling the wonderful story of God's love for us. After the service food and drink were served, and I was able to meet Joe's wife and other members of the congregation. Suddenly I felt at home. As Christians we have a family all over the world, and I knew that I was enfolded in the love of God wherever I was.

10

Execution and Reprieve

IN 1995 I HAD TAKEN ON my third pen-friend, though that wasn't exactly what I had planned. José had written to me saying that his cellmate Roberto would like to have an English pen-friend, but I didn't intend to take him on myself. I knew Roberto was from El Salvador and his first language was Spanish, and I planned to pass his name on to my friend Regina.

I first met Regina when she was playing the piano for rehearsals at my daughters' amateur dramatic society, and when I found that she, too, was interested in prison correspondence our friendship blossomed. Regina had been writing to a man called Geoffrey, who was on Death Row in Texas, and she had managed to go out and visit him only a few weeks before he was executed. His death had shaken her badly, and with my deepening friendship with Tommy I could understand how she must feel. Nevertheless I thought it would be good for her to get another pen-friend, and as she spoke good Spanish, I thought Roberto would be ideal. I finally convinced Regina to take him on by pointing out that she would not be faced with another death like Geoffrey's: Roberto, like José, was serving a life sentence in Pelican Bay, California.

However, only a few weeks later, Roberto was transferred to another institution, and José was temporarily alone. He was sorry to see Rob go, and apprehensive about gaining a new "cellie":

I have some bad news. Roberto is gone, 'n right now I'm by myself 'n waiting to see who is going to be my next cellmate. Hopefully someone comparable 'n I can get along with, so if your friend Regina post the letter for Roberto, is going to be a while before she gets a reply ... About the religious issue, I appreciate your advice, so I'm thinking of taking these studies as you said it might help by inhancing my knowledge, and perhaps in a sence I can get closer to God – also I want to thank you for those encouraging words – I want you to know that I feel the same about you and your daughters' friendship.

Inmates in America's jails are not allowed to communicate with other prisoners in different institutions, unless they are co-defendants on the same charge, in which case they may exchange information which could be of use to them in their appeals. Once Rob had gone from Pelican Bay, there was no way for José to contact him. The obvious way round such a problem is via a third party. So Regina also wrote to José to pass on messages from Roberto, and I also wrote to Roberto to pass on messages from José. In this way we could keep both of them in touch, and even pass on letters from one to the other, enclosed inside our own.

José was happy to hear how well Regina and Roberto were doing: "So Roberto is writing Regina still, and they are getting along pretty good, well when you see her again, give my regards to her and send my best to him and that I wish the [parole] board will give him a break, also how is the civil suit going?"

Pelican Bay is a tough place, and José would often give me a glimpse of conditions there. He was never self-pitying or defeatist, but at times his spirits were understandably low. He was always most appreciative when I tried to cheer him:

I want to thank you again for making me realize that my situation is not as bad, in fact it could be worst, it's a great example you gave me about the daughter of your friend Penny. I guess people in the circumstances like me needs to talk about it, because words of encouragement give us another push and made us fight against the odds. I thank God for having you to talk to about it.

In October 1997 he wrote to say that he had heard from Regina and that she and Rob were getting "real close":

I got a letter from Regina your friend. She wrote to say thanks, because I got her to write to Roberto, and for what she say they are getting along very good. I told her that you deserve most of the credit, because you were the one who decided to give her his name, and not somebody else, so I congratulate you for a good matching. She mentioned she will be coming to visit him soon, he is lucky dog!

Six years later, after several trips to California to see both José and Roberto, Regina married Rob. It was the first of several matches I made, and despite my misgivings about these relationships between prisoners and people on the outside, I was happy for them both. I even began to wonder if my deep friendship with Tommy was the start of something more significant, but he quickly disabused me of that idea: "I have nothing to offer you Penny. My future is uncertain. I can't ask you to sacrifice everything for me. I couldn't live with myself if I did that."

I spoke to Kaki, my pastor friend who had helped set up the Reconciliation organization in Nashville, and she too quickly quashed any such notion. "Tommy can do nothing for you, Penny," she wrote. I knew it was true, but I also believed that God didn't plan for me to be alone for the rest of my life. He had someone out there for me.

I told Tommy that I was thinking of moving to America,

but instead of being pleased or flattered, he was distressed: "Penny that would be the ultimate sacrifice ... and I just can't put you in that kind of situation because it would be tantamount to asking you to leave one prison only to enter another with me ... and it would be totally selfish of me."

His situation was still the same: years had passed and he was still on Death Row, never knowing whether the state would decide to end his life at any time. I threw myself into a frenzy of letter writing on his behalf, to lawyers, legislators and even the President's wife. I cited the case of the Bird Man of Alcatraz, Robert Stroud, whose mother went to see the President's wife to plead for her son's life.

Meanwhile José's case had come up before the parole board, so I wrote to them too, giving him a glowing character witness and hoping that they might move him to a less hostile environment. They thanked me politely for my letters, and said that they would be noted. Nothing came of my efforts on that occasion.

I was trying to get to grips with the complexities of the American legal system – although it was originally based on our own, it is now totally different. I had learned that men on the Row spend much of their time researching their own cases and writing their own appeals, since the official legal representation they are offered is usually so inadequate. Whenever I visited I was always amazed at the amount of legal information the men had at their fingertips, as they became their own lawyers and advocates.

In Tommy's case it was hard to know how to proceed. He was keeping his head down, doing his time, and keeping out of trouble. Sometimes it felt as though if only we all kept quiet, he might escape the notice of the state – certainly there was no sign that anyone was agitating to have him executed immediately. Perhaps it was best to let things lie. On the other hand, the political climate in the USA was not a good one for him. The media devoted a great deal of time and space to debates about crime and punishment, whipping up a frenzy of public anxiety, and encouraging demands for deterrent sentences. Attitudes were hardening and things looked likely to get worse. Surely we should try to move Tommy's case forward, before the "fry 'em" element won the day.

On several occasions I had watched political shows on American television, and I was horrified by the general attitude to crime and punishment. I could discern no difference between Republicans and Democrats – they all seemed to be hard-liners with extreme views. Of course, the truth of the matter was that all the politicians were vote-catching, and they wanted to appear tough on crime. One Democratic candidate described the fact that a man had been on Death Row awaiting execution for sixteen years as "cruel and unusual punishment" – the very words the Supreme Court had used to describe execution itself, when it suspended capital punishment in 1972. (Four years later it overturned this ruling, and thirty-eight states promptly reinstated the death penalty.) This man's concern rang hollow when it became clear that he was simply advocating a speedier route to the final end.

Another candidate demanded that the lengthy appeal process should be shortened. Again, he tried to appear reasonable and civilized, implying that in this way some men would get off the Row faster, when he really wanted the state to get on with killing them. One Republican really enraged me. He insisted that the courts were extremely reluctant to impose death sentences because of their finality, and tried to convince his audience that therefore all the people under sentence of death must deserve it. I knew this was a downright lie, and I fumed to think how many people would swallow it whole, just as I once had, and put their trust unquestioningly in a system of justice that could never be infallible.

Ending up on the Row, I knew, was entirely a matter of luck. It was determined by your colour, your income, the race of the victim, the location of the crime, the selection of the jury, the zeal of the District Attorney and the quality of your legal representation. In an offence of homicide, the death penalty was most likely to be imposed if the offender was black and the victim white – and least likely to be imposed if both were black. Many of the more northern states of the Union had no death penalty, so similar offences could result in entirely different punishments in places just a couple of miles apart.

The death penalty in America is capricious and random; it is disproportionately applied to minorities and the poor. It allows no room for redemption, takes no account of change in a person's heart, and it is ultimately final and irreversible. I wondered what I would do if I were ever asked to witness an execution. How could I watch my friend die? But how could I refuse, and let a friend leave this life without me by his side? I couldn't bear to think about it. Even hearing about an execution from the other side of the Atlantic was traumatic enough.

I met Glen through an advert he had placed in a magazine column entitled "Prisoners seeking pen-friends" – he said he loved books, poetry and creative writing. I wrote to him and learned that he was a young man barely out of his teens, black and gay. I wasn't surprised that he had ended up on Death Row. However, some Rows are worse than others, as some states are much more eager to impose the death penalty than others. Glen's prison, Huntsville, was in Texas, which is as bad as it gets. Texas leads all the other states in the number of executions carried out.

December 27th 1995. Dearest Penny, Greetings, peace, living and solidarity ... may this letter indeed find your person doing well and in good health. I have just received your letter and must say that I was delighted to hear from you ... as I was not aware that there was individuals whom was interested in responding to my ad in a quest of receiving a pen-friends, however nobody responded but you – it's been months.

He described himself in some detail and went on to tell me he was reading Maya Angelou's *I Know Why the Caged Bird Sings*, a book I had also read fairly recently. He was ecstatic about it, and listed for me many other titles he had enjoyed. His father had just died, and he was trying to scrape together some money to enable his mother to travel to the jail to visit him. She was an unstable woman with many problems of her own, and Glen's relationship with her had been difficult.

His letters always began with the same salutation:

Greetings, peace, living and solidarity ... I have you know that I have just received your letter this afternoon, and therefore would like to take this moment to thank you very much for the temporary insight you have given my person allowing me to share part of your world for the time that it has taken your person to gather your thoughts together for my person.

I just wrote my mother as I have just received a letter from her person, and throughout her whole letter she was stressing the fact that times are so hard, she was going to give an extra effort in trying to come to terms with her life, the fact that she is in an annex building rehabilitation center, about to make release and has no where to go disturbs my person in ways it's hard comprehend to self, so trying to find the right words to relay this feeling will only succeed in the undervaluing of the reality of the situation, therefore I refrain.

He wrote fondly of his grandmother:

You inquires about my grandmother, yes she does visits me when she can, she has come recently as my birthday was right around the corner, however, I cannot tell you when I will see her again, it's just important to me that she knows that she is loved and appreciated before she comes and after she leaves, as nothing is guaranteed, and knowing a love is visiting Utopian image of heaven, but on earth ... she is really a classy lady in her own right, where as dignity holds the key to determining the quality of a being in the manner which effort is giving in the handling of self.

To tell the truth, I found Glen hard going at times. His handwriting was tricky to decipher and his thoughts were often rambling. He seemed to withdraw into his own private world, and I felt that I was unable to reach him. I know he valued our friendship, though:

I believe in my heart that you are a good person, you have a beautiful heart ... I thank you for attempting to be part of my life ... I have you know that you are in my thoughts ... I would have you know however all my shortcomings, that I do thank you for being whom you are, and I thank you for all your prayers and your thoughts where I am concerned, thanks a lot!

Glen was my pen-friend for just five years. Before his execution he had been worrying about his burial – he was anxious to avoid being laid to rest within the prison compound. I felt powerless to be of any help at such a distance, but I did manage to telephone a few contacts and put him in touch with them, in the hope that they might have some suggestions that would ease his mind. Glen had come to the end of the road with his appeals, and I knew that the date for his execution had been set, but prisoners often receive a temporary stay at the eleventh hour, only to have that stay lifted some days or weeks later.

This time it didn't happen. The State of Texas exacted its punishment on 25 January 2000.

Six days after Glen died, I received a thank-you card from him, written just hours before his end. He expressed his gratitude for my friendship over the years. It was an eerie and uncomfortable feeling to be reading the words of a dead man, especially as I considered that I had never really got to know the troubled young man, or been able to help him as I would have wished.

Fortunately not everyone on Death Row ends up in the execution chamber. Harmon once asked me to accompany him to the Federal Court where his friend Bill's appeal was being heard. Bill had been found guilty of murder, and the victim's sister had arranged for the media to cover the proceedings. Outside the courthouse there were ranks of vans and pantechnicons bearing the CNN logo, and reporters milled around on the pavement. A crowd of death-penalty supporters waved banners demanding Bill's execution, and a handful of us stood apart, wearing our badges saying "Don't kill in my name".

We took our seats at the back of the courtroom – twelve of us among a room full of people determined to see the death penalty enforced. When Bill was brought in by a guard, he looked small and frail in his oversized orange boiler suit. He turned briefly to acknowledge our presence with a weak smile.

We soon realized that Bill was lucky – he was appearing before the one judge on the circuit who didn't support the killing machine unquestioningly, and who was bent on hearing all sides of the argument. He was a small man with a shock of white hair who sat hunched in his chair and at times appeared to be asleep, but then he would fire out some question which indicated that a razor-sharp intellect was perfectly in command of the court. It was a masterful performance, and very exciting to watch. The scene was so familiar to anyone who has seen courtroom dramas on TV or at the cinema, that I had to remind myself that this was real, and a man's life depended on the outcome. The American legal system moves very slowly, but after a few months Bill was taken off the Row, and moved back to a prison near his home town of Memphis to serve out his sentence.

Blue was another man who had gained relief from the lengthy appeals procedure, and had his sentence commuted to life imprisonment. I had noticed him on my very first visit to Riverbend – a middle-aged, thick-set black man with greying hair, sweeping up in the reception area. He chatted cheerily to the visitors, leaning on his broom and exchanging a few pleasantries with everyone who passed through. He always asked me about the girls, how they were doing and when they would be coming with me next. He was especially interested in England since his niece had visited the country with her church, and he was full of questions.

Blue had almost served out his life sentence, and as a "trustee" he was allowed to live on the prison farm about half a mile away. Eight prisoners were bussed in every morning in their prison uniforms to work in the grounds and reception area, trimming the lawns and keeping the place tidy. The others were rather more reserved and wary, but Blue was a sociable character who loved to talk.

One day he bounced up to me, grinning. "Hey, missy Penny," he said, "Guess what? I got my parole! I'm goin' home next month!"

I grinned back and congratulated him heartily. A flicker of regret crossed his face, and he said, "I won't be here next time you come. Promise you'll write to me?"

I promised that I would, if he gave me his address as soon as he had his housing arranged. I scribbled my own address on a scrap of paper and gave it to him.

A few weeks later, I heard that he was staying in a half-way house for five months, while he got used to functioning in the outside world once more. He wrote me a brief note saying that he wasn't really a great writer, and asked if we could exchange cassette tapes instead. I duly mailed a cassette tape to him, and received one back soon after. He told me that he would leave the reverse side of the tape blank, so that I could record my message and return it to him. However, when I turned the tape over I found that he was still speaking – and in typical garrulous Blue fashion, he went on and on. In fact, the tape ran out with him still in mid-sentence!

He told me a lot about his offence, which he committed as a very young man. He had spent a couple of years on Death Row before his appeal was heard and his sentence was altered to life imprisonment. He then spent a further twenty-nine years in prison. He said that of the handful of men released at the same time as him, all but one had committed other petty crimes and gone straight back inside. He was doing well with his own home, a truck and two part-time jobs. So far, though, he said, he hadn't found himself a wife!

I met others who had been reprieved like Blue. At one meeting I attended, we were addressed by a group of ten men wearing T-shirts bearing the words "Don't Follow Me". They were ex-offenders who visited schools and young offenders' institutions to give their personal testimonies, talk about drug abuse, and try to prevent young people from following them into a life of crime. Two of them had started out on Death Row, but they were trying to turn their lives around and make a positive contribution to society. I wished the reporters and banner-wavers who demanded death could have met them; perhaps they could begin to see what a waste of life the death penalty is.

11

Understanding Anger

I T WASN'T ALWAYS EASY to correspond with prisoners. Tommy was unusual in the degree of self-awareness he had attained, his humility, and in his ability to control his emotions and to deal with the situation he found himself in. I found it easy to relate to him, but I had other penfriends with whom it was more difficult to sustain a friendship.

I first heard about Errol in a totally unexpected letter, which came from an address in America which I didn't recognize. Someone I didn't know – Nicole – wrote that she had heard about me, and knew that I cared about people in prison. Her friend Errol was on Death Row in Missouri; she believed him to be innocent of the murder of a middle-aged woman, and was convinced that there was DNA evidence that would clear him. She begged me to contact him. I prayed and thought about it, and eventually decided to write to Errol – but he turned out to be a difficult character.

Greetings! My name is Errol and I received your letter just moments ago and it's always a pleasure to hear from anyone who is willing to listen and offer moral support. In all honesty I respect you for that because society has a very dim outlook upon those who have been sentenced to death for heinous crimes, regardless if they are in fact innocent. It seems as if the majority of your time is spent on listening to the problems of those less fortunate who really have nothing to offer you in return.

He went on to describe himself and mentioned Nicole:

> My spirits have been broken, my reputation defamed and more importantly my friends have turned to foes. The only friend I would even consider as such ... is Nicole and we have two children, one who will be twenty in December and one who will be seven in February ... Penny, I thank you for writing to me and I hope to hear from you again ... peace and love, sincerely, Errol.

Errol, like Tommy, was black and had been convicted by an all-white jury. Unlike Tommy, he was a Muslim and a devotee of Louis Farakhan and the Nation of Islam, a religious movement which favours racial segregation and promotes anti-Semitism. Errol thought of himself as a charmer, and would often flirt in an innocent way: "Many men would beg, borrow and even steal to have enough money to take you out for a night on the town."

He was capable of great mood swings, and his anger and frustration could lead him to hit out at anyone, including me. He had fallen out with several of his defence team, various prison officials and even Nicole. After one particularly hurtful letter I began to consider quite seriously whether I really wanted to carry on with our correspondence. However, I reflected, I had undertaken to see things through to the bitter end with all my friends, so really I had no choice. In any case, Errol never stayed angry for long: after a note full of abuse and vituperation, the next would be apologetic and ask forgiveness. Being Errol's pen-friend was an emotional roller-coaster.

All my correspondents knew that I wrote to several

other people besides themselves, though I never discussed them or their cases in detail. Privacy, tact and confidentiality are essential requirements for anyone embarking on pen-friendships with inmates. However, I did once confide that one of "my guys" had been hurtful and verbally abusive. Their reaction was universally direct and unequivocal: get rid of him. Tommy, Roberto and José were all of the same opinion on this subject:

> What are you thinking of, writing to a man like that?
>
> About your friend ... I would not know how to start and finish a letter to a person like him ... it sound like you are dealing with a kid ... I pray that he never disrespect you in any way.
>
> I am sorry for the way this other pen-pal of yours treated you, and as I said before, there is no reason to act that way towards someone who takes time to care, and give moral support, for the simple fact that it's not your fault that he is where he is ... you are only trying to show compassion, but he is taking it for granted, the Death Row is the place to learn how to be patient, recognize that those who write during this hard time, they should treasure instead of pressure, so my advice in this case is to let him go, this cause is lost, so it is time to move on and let him be with his misery, which is exactly what he wants.

I told them that Errol would always come back penitent in his letter, but José for one wasn't convinced:

> So this guy wrote you back and apologized in a birthday card he sent you and if I'm not mistaking this is not the first time he does this in fact you mentioned that he had done the same a couple of years or so ago and as I said then, you are a better person when it comes to giving this guy another chance, after all these years I've come to know those who really appreciate the friendship of pen-pals and those who only want something from them.

I wasn't willing to give up, though. I realized that men like Errol were used to being let down time and time again, and I didn't want to be one of those who did so. He was unable to control the anger and frustration he felt in his precarious situation, and if he was indeed innocent, it was understandable that at times he would hit out at anyone with whom he came into contact. Christian love wasn't about giving up on people; it was about holding on no matter what, and seeking no thanks.

In any case, I was convinced that Errol did appreciate our friendship in his own way – otherwise, why would he be such a regular and consistent correspondent? No one was making him write to me. If he wanted anything other than simple companionship he would have given up long before, when he realized that this was all I had to offer.

I decided that Errol was a test of my resolve and commitment. He made me re-examine my motives for staying involved in this activity. It's easy to respond to those who appreciate our efforts; most of us bond most readily with those who pay us attention and bolster our sense of self-worth. I knew that I had gained a great deal from some of my prisoner friends who had done just that for me – but that was certainly not my prime reason for my prison friendships. I really believed that Jesus had instructed us to care for the lonely, the outcast and the prisoner, and this was my way of following him. I decided that God wanted me to persist with my friendship with Errol, whatever advice I had to the contrary: "So, he think he is the master charmer and that he will win you over and keep you wrap round his little finger. Well he is in for a long haul if he think that, I know you are a better judge of character than that."

There were sometimes signs in Errol's letters that he was beginning to come to terms with himself:

I feel bad because I didn't abuse Nicole physically but I will admit that I did abuse her mentally by constantly running around with undesirable women who would stop at nothing to break us up. Yeah, I was nothing but a male courtesan to put it mildly and that seems to bother me in the worst way. I almost caused the woman of my dreams to commit suicide and if I had went to work as planned she would have been dead when I returned.

His remorse was inconsistent though. Not long after he had written these words of regret he was back to talking about Nicole dismissively. I had told him about some writing I was doing: "Surely, if Nicole can write a book then I know you can because, in my eyes she's as dense as a box of rocks. Sad, but true."

On another occasion he told me about some art work he had done: "I just finished a portrait of Nicole, our children and myself and she hasn't even taken the time to write and say thanks. I can't stand an ungrateful person and I think it's time I drop her a line and let her know that."

He told me that he had had a visit from his young son, but when I asked how it had gone, his reply was full of anger:

Yes, I had a good visit with Angelo, at least I tried to. Nicole is such a bitch that I despise her. Yeah, she came out with an attitude and told me that she wanted off my visiting list because she was on someone else's, therefore who will bring my son to see me. I haven't seen him in five years and then she pulls a stunt like that, huh. If I weren't a Muslim striving to stay on the right path, I'd send someone to see her, and trust me it wouldn't be anything nice.

He worried about Angelo now that Nicole was having a relationship with another prisoner:

> To put Angelo in the middle is pretty low. She must be doing awful bad ... so many men on the street and she falls for one in prison after a failed marriage for the third time. For all I know this man could be a pedophile ... she's so stupid ... she said he got ten years for robbery and murder. That's not possible. The robbery along with armed criminal action carries three to life and then murder. I don't think so.

He had other problems too. He broke his ankle badly in the exercise yard, but the prison medical service was inadequate, and it was slow to heal. "It hurts so bad that I can't stand to set in this position for long periods of time – so this may be short!" Over a year later it was still troubling him: "Yes, I'm still having trouble with my leg and kicking fifty-yard field goals isn't helping it either. When kicking that football it feels like a brick has landed on my foot, but as always, no pain, no gain!"

He was also worried about his sixteen-year-old relative Victor, who was in danger of joining him on the Row. Victor had been charged with the murder of a family member, and Errol was convinced that the prosecutors were trying to stall the trial until the boy was eighteen so that they could try him as an adult and therefore press for the death sentence.

Errol distrusted almost everyone in authority. Many of his letters would be accompanied by newspaper cuttings with headlines like "State's High Court chides judge for racial remark", "Senator is called racist" and "Illinois Republican criticized minorities". He referred to "Amerikka" and "the United Snakes of America" and believed he was a victim of racism and would never get a fair trial in such a country. Even his defence team came in for attack: "I thank you for contacting my attorney, but for some reason demonstrated to me by him, I feel that he won't write back. He is one arrogant SOB that I despise him with a passion."

I wrote on Errol's behalf to Centurion Ministries, a Christian organization set up by a church pastor to help victims of miscarriages of justice. Like all such groups they were run on a shoestring, but they had a good record of getting death sentences overturned on appeal. They replied that they knew of Errol's case already. "Thank you for your letter on behalf of Mr —, your pen-pal. Mr — wrote to us in 1995 and never responded to our return correspondence. However, if he cares to pursue his case, please encourage him to write to us at the address on this letterhead. Thanks for your interest in the innocent incarcerated."

Errol had convinced himself that they were shysters, paying lip-service to the truth; perhaps he believed that no help would come from that quarter because they were Christians and he was a Muslim. I felt sorry for him, because I could see how difficult he made life for himself. He had asked me several times to find him a second pen-friend, but finding people willing to commit to a long-term and often trying correspondence was tricky. Many of my friends were already writing to several prisoners, and I knew that Beryl, an experienced LifeLiner, had already had problems with Errol; I felt it was unfair to bring anyone else into such a situation.

Fortunately Geraldine was willing to take him on, and she was steadfast and reliable. She was a remarkable lady in her eighties, from a neighbouring state. She wrote to Errol and even visited him whenever she could, in spite of her health problems. I met her twice and we got on well; she kept me in touch with developments in Errol's case as she made strenuous appeals to his lawyers and to senators on his behalf. She encouraged him with telephone calls and even sent him small gifts.

Errol was often in trouble with the prison authorities for minor conduct violations, and he would fume about it in his letters to me: "They're recommending that I be placed in Administrative Segregation for a conduct violation I received on the 20th for allegedly passing an unknown object in another housing unit as well as supposedly telling the officer F*** YOU. Man, these people aint shit. I hate every last one of these racist hillbilllies."

At times he could be witty and charming, and though he loved to flirt, he never overstepped the mark or became offensive or coarse. When I had the chance to speak to him on the telephone he was bright and obviously pleased to speak to me. What a strange mixture he was! Full of contradictions, never predictable or boring, Errol could be relied on to keep me on my toes. "Listen, I don't want to destroy the essence of this missive so I'm going to say this to you on your special day. 'When I try to express your worth no words seem capable; for in you is the essence of life.' May all your days be filled with peace!" It was a combined birthday and Mother's Day greeting.

> Greetings Babygirl! I received your most welcome missive and you're right, it was a surprise because I didn't recognize the writing, but once I saw the return address I figured it had to be you. Smile! As always it's a pleasure hearing from you … I thank you for the stamps as well as your trying to contact the person who investigates miscarriages of justice. I do hope you find him and quick before my time runs out.

I tried to make allowances for Errol's violent and unpredictable mood swings, and I came to the conclusion that the only way to do it was to try to imagine what it must be like to be in his situation. For one thing, he was living under the strain of the constant threat of execution which was part of life on Death Row. The "top" three states in the Death Row league – that is, the ones who most actively pursue a policy of clearing the prisons of men convicted of capital murder by putting them to death as rapidly as possible – are Texas, Florida and Missouri. Missouri was doing its best to stay in the top three: in 1996 it had put five men to death, including three in the month of August. Errol had described to me the atmosphere in the unit when a "brother" was taken down to the death cell to spend his final hours and eat his last meal. He vowed that when his time came, he wouldn't go without a fight.

Then there was the everyday monotony of life in prison, with the confinement in a tiny cell and the restrictions of endless rules, enlivened only by outbreaks of violence among the prisoners. Added to this there was the stress of an undercurrent of racism. Errol sent me a copy of a letter found on the bed of a young black man held in a Chicago city jail. It was signed "a faithful Klansman" and contained encouragement to "go pull a trigger on a nigger". It was hard to grasp what it must be like to live among such hatred and bigotry. I decided that Errol needed all the friends he could get.

It was difficult for me to comprehend how common racism was in everyday life in America, but I did have one or two experiences on the outside which gave me some insight. On one visit my friend Frances picked me up from the airport in her Volvo, and drove to the exit booth only to find that she had lost the parking ticket. The attendant was becoming impatient, so Frances reversed to allow other cars to pass while we searched for the ticket. When we found it she was in a hurry to get going.

"Let's get out of here quick," she said. "They're quite

likely to call the cops if they see a black woman driving a nice car, if she doesn't seem to know what she's doing."

"Why?" I asked.

"They'll assume it's stolen, of course," she replied. It was the last thing that would have occurred to me: Frances was a confident, well-educated woman, well-dressed and articulate, who held down a responsible job with IBM, the computer company. How could anyone assume that she was a thief?

Later in the same week I had another powerful illustration of her fear of racism. Frances agreed to drive me to my friend Shirley's home, to buy a book she had written about her son Jeff who was on Death Row. Shirley lived on a trailer park, where road names weren't much in evidence, and in the dark it wasn't easy to distinguish which mobile home was which. They were all on rough grass plots surrounded by wire fencing, but we couldn't see any numbers or other identification. Eventually we figured out which home was Shirley's and I got out of the car and waited for Frances to follow. Several large and ferocious dogs were prowling round inside the yard, growling and barking at us. Frances wound down the window.

"I'll wait in the car," she said. "This isn't the sort of neighbourhood a black woman wants to be out in at night."

There was genuine fear in her voice, and for one brief moment I glimpsed what it must be like to be black in the southern states of America. Even after all these years, and despite the civil rights movement, for some, both in the North and the South, attitudes have changed very little.

I was beginning to see that the USA has its own culture, which because of its different history is very different from the culture of the United Kingdom. It helped me to understand some of Errol's anger and the despair of his situation.

12

Not Just a Number

DURING ONE OF MY VISITS to Tennessee an execution took place in another state. The man in question was English by birth; the British press had covered the story in some detail, and both the Prime Minister and religious leaders had appealed for his life to be spared. At the time I was a regular contributor to my local radio station, where the head of religious broadcasting had become a friend. Radio Stoke set up a live satellite link to interview me and to gauge American public opinion. Sadly, I had to tell them that the US press and TV had no interest in the man or his circumstances, and that state executions were so commonplace that they simply didn't make the news any more.

It seemed to me that few Americans had much interest in the way things were done in the rest of the world, and neither did they bother about how their activities were viewed. If they thought about it at all, I suspected that their attitude would have been dismissive. "So what if the guy's English? He's a convicted felon who ended up on Death Row over here. He pays the price according to our rules. It'll be one less villain in the world."

This made me think about the media representation of the death penalty. I am old enough to remember a time before it was abolished in England; I have vague memories of hangings in the late 1950s and early 1960s. However, to people younger than myself the death penalty seems archaic and alien: for them it often has a morbid fascination. In Britain there is an appetite for salacious details of executions, but in the USA there is little interest.

One case was an exception. In the early hours of the morning of 10 May 1994, John Wayne Gacy was executed by lethal injection at Stateville Prison, Illinois, after spending fourteen years on Death Row. Unfortunately an intravenous drip malfunctioned during the proceedings and he took some considerable time to die, which was distressing for the execution squad and the onlookers, and raised some questions in the press.

Gacy was America's worst ever serial killer, having been found guilty of the murder of thirty-three young men and boys. In a country where homicide rates are high, the sheer number of his crimes was shocking. Many people believe that Death Row is full of people like Gacy, but they are wrong. The Charles Mansons, the Jeffrey Dahmers and the John Gacys are the exceptions not the rule. Those of us who work in this field try hard to overcome such prejudices and misconceptions.

A young reporter covering the story for British television let slip a telling comment. When she was asked what she thought was the average American citizen's view of executions, she answered: "Some people would advocate life without parole rather than letting them die." The use of the word "letting" was interesting. It implied that society was doing the men a favour by permitting them to escape from their monotonous and meaningless existence.

Gacy's case raised two objections to the death penalty. First, the fact that Gacy spent fourteen years behind bars between his sentencing and his death means that the punishment is detached from the crime for which it is handed down. If the sentence is meant to be a deterrent, then a speedier administration of justice would make more sense, when the memory of the crime is fresh in the mind of the public, and the punishment can be seen to follow a finding of guilt. As it is, the long delay means that the crime has faded from the public awareness, and the execution of another prisoner means little.

Secondly, the malfunction of the equipment meant that his death was not even quick and merciful. Because of such technical failures, many people favour life without parole as an alternative to state execution.

How do we form our opinions? I believe that it is from a combination of learning from authority and our own experiences. We believe that a plane will fly, even though we ourselves have no understanding of the laws of aerodynamics – and we have seen aeroplanes do so, reliably and safely. We believe that the earth is part of the solar system, even though we ourselves have not experienced space travel, and may not have access to a radio telescope. We pick up information from trusted authorities, and believe it because it accords with our own limited observations. Sometimes we modify our beliefs in the light of personal experience. One friend of mine always held very strong opinions on the subject of divorce – but she subsequently modified these views when her own daughter's marriage failed, and she saw at close hand how difficult it was to apportion blame.

All the arguments and theories about capital punishment (and indeed about crime and punishment in general) become irrelevant when you know someone as an individual, and understand their history, the circumstances surrounding their offending and the situation they find themselves in. Developing a deep friendship with someone on the other side of the bars forces you to abandon all your assumptions and preconceptions.

This was my experience time and time again as I made contact with prisoners and a real relationship began to develop between us. Crimes which seem horrific when you first hear of them – usually in the cold language of the court which pronounced sentence – may seem very different when you hear about them from the point of view of the prisoner. This is not to say that the befriender must be gullible and easily deceived: it is possible to take an objective view of the facts. Nor should we become familiarized with or hardened to the effects of crime, or forget the effects on the victim. It's simply that understanding a person as an individual makes a great difference to one's ideas about punishment.

Tommy was a good example. He had been sentenced to death for homicide, yet he knew that he had acted in self-defence. He acknowledged and accepted his guilt, and was filled with remorse that he had taken the life of another man – yet US law allows for degrees of culpability. If he had been properly defended in court, other aspects of his case might have been revealed. Tommy's situation was more complex than the bald statement "sentenced to death for homicide" would suggest.

In 1997 I watched a TV documentary about women on the Row. It featured three in particular, and outlined the crimes they had committed. One woman stood out for me: she struck me as a bubbly, likeable type, and I decided to try to contact her. That was how my friendship with Angela began.

I received your most welcomed letter a couple of months ago and it was a real joy to hear from you. It is my sincere prayer that these few lines will reach you and all your family in good health and in perfect spiritual peace ... please forgive my long delay in answering but it could not be helped. I had not stamps and when I was able to get one then I hurt my writing hand but it is healed now and I am able to write. No, I don't mind you're writing to me, as a matter of fact it is a joy to get your letter. I do hope that you will continue to write to me. I would love for us to stay in touch. You have been writing to prisoners for a very long time. Were you able to visit the man who got out of prison in England? I do not get visits from my sons as it's too expensive ... I am over an eight hour drive from them ... I have been on Death Row for thirteen and half years now, since February 1984 but I pray things will change for me this year – needless to say I am tired of being here but it's a lot better than being dead.

She sent me a list of things she was allowed to receive through the post, and I immediately forwarded some stamps, to keep our newly established friendship on track.

Angela was a black woman, found guilty of killing a cop – one of only around thirty women in the country who had been given the maximum sentence. She was on Death Row in Florida. It seemed a grim situation to me, but Angela was always up-beat and optimistic about her chances, and eventually she was proved right. She sent me copies of letters she had received from her legal team, which encouraged her optimism: "The oral argument went very well. There were no surprises from the State, and I think our position is clear to the justices. Of course, there is no way to predict how or when the court will rule. But I came away from the argument with a favorable impression of our chances of success."

Her other attorney was equally positive: "I don't want to count any chickens, but the argument went very well. Bill M was very well prepared, and did an outstanding job ... So now we wait. I'd say keep praying, but I know you will anyway."

Angela continued to be hopeful: "The Governor ... let about six people off of Death Row not too far back and commuted their sentences. Most of them went free. God is still on the throne – Amen." In June 1999 she wrote:

I received your card and stamps and letter and I was blessed and overjoyed to hear from you. It is my sincere prayer that these few lines will reach you in good health and in perfect spiritual peace, living by faith. Please find enclosed one photo of me. I hope it will bless you. I am sorry this is the only one I have.

Her next letter was to be the last one I received from Death Row.

I am glad you liked and enjoyed the photo I sent to you ... My appeal was filed on 1/28/99 but it will be at the end of the year before we hear anything. I saw my family (my youngest son and my siblings) in January 99. I hope to see them again in June, so do let me know how the LifeLines conference goes, OK?

All her faith and hope was well founded. She left Death Row shortly afterwards.

Please except my apologies for not writing sooner but it was unavoidable as I was out to court *again* on my case. I am fine and I give God all the glory and the praise ... I am now in school studying to get my Associates degree in computer/electronic repair. All I do now is just study and pray!

Like Blue, Angela was one of the lucky ones. Jeff, the son of my friend Shirley, was less fortunate. He insisted that he was innocent, but the court refused to believe him.

Jeff's story was that he had become friends with a man called Chief, who was supposedly looking for work. He moved in with Jeff, but he never showed any sign of getting a job. One day the two men drove into town and stopped in the main street. Chief said he was going to rob a store, but Jeff didn't believe him. He stayed in the car, and it was only when Chief came out, covered in blood, that Jeff realized he had been serious – he had killed the store owner. There were several witnesses to identify him as the murderer, and Chief was soon arrested; Jeff and his mother Shirley went on the run.

Chief refused to speak up for Jeff, and when he was picked up too, bail was set high. Shirley and her family had no way of raising it, so they tried to help him break out of jail. The attempt failed, and Jeff was moved to Brushy Mountain prison, where security was tight. At the trial, Chief still refused to admit that Jeff had been outside in the car during the murder. In US law, an accomplice at the scene is equally guilty, and Jeff found himself convicted of capital murder.

> My mother was taken out of the courtroom by the sheriff because she yelled out during the argument. She was trying to tell the jurors that I had not taken part in the murder and the judge yelled for the sheriff to put her in jail. It tore me up to see the pain she was going through and I wished there was something that I could do for her.

I had met Shirley the first time I travelled to America. She had sold her house and almost everything she owned to pay for Jeff's legal defence, and she was living on a trailer park about thirty miles from the prison where he was held. She had written several books about the case and the death penalty in general, so she was well known in the campaigning circles in which I was moving. All the guys in prison knew her too, because she always supplied little parcels of Christmas goodies for the ones who had no friends or relations to send them. She was also bringing up Jeff's daughter Maria, because Jeff's young wife could not care for the child herself.

Whenever I was in the USA I would meet Shirley for lunch somewhere. I could see that her health was deteriorating – the stress was too much for her, her nerves were shot to pieces, and each time I visited she was on a bigger and more terrifying cocktail of drugs. Jeff wasn't faring much better. He was found to have a serious heart problem, no doubt brought on by, or at least exacerbated by his years in prison.

In May 1999 Jeff died, aged forty-one, of a massive heart attack. The state did not execute him, but inadequate prison healthcare no doubt contributed to his early demise. Jeff's case wasn't unusual. Many inmates become physically ill on Death Row, and many more suffer from serious mental health problems as a direct result of the strain of living with their death hanging over them every day.

Jeff died before his case had run through the full (lengthy) appeals procedure. The fact that many of those on Death Row have their sentences commuted on appeal or are even proved innocent is a powerful argument against the death penalty. It is utterly irrevocable and mistakes can never be rectified. Those of us who get to know prisoners are often baffled and frustrated by our inability to persuade the legal system to explore their cases in sufficient detail. Of course, we are the more frustrated because we have built up real relationships with these people – we no longer see them as numbers on a list, cases in a court, or caricatures of criminals. To us they are real, warm human beings with lives, loves, needs, interests and valuable qualities of their own.

This goes some way towards explaining how it sometimes comes about that pen-friends become romantically involved, and decide to take the enormous step of marriage with prisoners. I once took part in a discussion programme produced by a satellite TV company. The show was called *Live Wire*, and it included an audience phone-in, when viewers could put their questions to a group of us who were involved in making contact with American criminals. The producer was expecting some hostile reactions, and I knew I needed to be careful and not allow myself to be goaded into saying something detrimental to our cause.

I travelled down to the studio in Bristol, and was pleased to find that as well as John, the presenter, and three other panel members, I was to meet Jan Arriëns, the man who founded the LifeLines organization. We all sat round a small table in a studio lined with monitors, and John spoke to each of us in turn about how we came to be involved with Death Row prisoners. There was a telephone interview with an English girl, educated and articulate, who had married her prisoner pen-friend and was now living in the USA. Jan was adamant that the organization did not promote romantic involvement with inmates.

"We are not a dating agency," he said emphatically, "but it sometimes happens, and it is not our job to forbid such things." He acknowledged that this particular young woman was thoughtful and knew her own mind, but he was still fiercely opposed to writers becoming emotionally entangled with their pen-friends. He explained how vulnerable and lonely the prisoners are, and how unfair it is to risk letting them down. He knew of one man who had been jilted by his fiancée when his appeal failed, and who had suffered a heart attack soon afterwards. Jan was deeply disturbed by the suggestion that the failure of this relationship had been a second trauma which contributed to his condition, and he was anxious to distance LifeLines from such behaviour. I respected him for the evident depth of his concern.

I was particularly concerned about the marriage of my friend Regina to Roberto, who was in prison in California. The responsibility for putting Rob and Regina in touch with each other weighed heavily upon me. The relationship had brought great joy and renewed hope to Rob, but I knew that life would be tough for Regina, being married to a man from a different culture, on a different continent, with very different life experiences. In prison, he could do little to help her. She would have to be the strong, active partner, and would need all the help her friends could give her.

"By the time this letter reaches your hands you will know that I got married with my sweet Regina on Friday ... thanks Penny for letting me know your good friend." A few weeks later he wrote another note: "Penny, my life was like a dry leaf for a while. I bounced around so much that I did not know where I would end up. But now it looks like I am in a more stable situation and little by little getting control of my life again."

Naturally, visits with his family and his new wife were times of high excitement and emotion, but even this new relationship didn't stop Rob's enthusiasm for keeping in touch: "Penny, Regina told me she had a nice time with you. I wish that you two could get to see each other more often. I know that she loves you like a sister."

At other times things were not so good, when Rob's hopes for his appeal were dashed, or when the atmosphere inside the jail was more than usually tense.

> Thanks for keeping me always in your thoughts and prayers. You know what I like about my situation, I like the feeling that the troubles in our lives ... its like it open ourselves more easy to God in the time of prayers ... I wish I could control this feeling and pray to God the way I am doing it now, all the time, but this anguish only come to us when we are facing life and death situation.

Such a partnership, with one on the inside and one on the outside, was never going to be easy. Yet why should we assume that these men must forgo all close relationships – marriage and friendship alike – just because they are paying their debt to society?

13

A Prisoner in Zambia

AFTER MY DIVORCE I had thrown myself into various activities – my creative writing, my letters to prisoners and my music – with renewed vigour. I was lonely, of course, but I had been equally lonely inside my marriage, and I was determined not to feel sorry for myself. Music was especially important to me: it was one of the paths I had found that led me closer to God, and listening to worship songs on a CD always lightened my mood. I had always loved singing in choirs at school and college, and I was an active member of the music group at Christ Church in Stone.

Our choir was a close-knit group, with eight or nine regular members who helped to lead the worship on Sundays, accompanied by three or four instrumentalists. We enjoyed each other's company and had a lot of fun: on one occasion I was elected as unofficial "shop steward" to try to maintain order in the ranks, and also to negotiate fair rates of pay when we turned out to sing at weddings – the usual rate being a princely £1 per person! We also rallied round with prayer and practical help if any of our members was ill or in need.

In January 1997 one of our members, Colin, told us the devastating news that his wife Margaret had been diagnosed with liver cancer. They had been married for almost forty years. Her illness was mercifully short: Margaret died three months later. After a short break Colin came back to our practices, finding comfort in the music and in the fellowship and support of old friends.

Several of my church friends lived alone because they were widowed or divorced, and I sometimes invited them to join me for lunch. Eventually I invited Colin, and we had a wonderful time together. Although we had known each other for twenty years, we had never spent time alone together, and we found we had lots of common interests and plenty to talk about. Colin was chairman of the local branch of the Children's Society, and took his charitable work very seriously, so he understood how important my work with prisoners was to me.

We began to go out for weekend walks around the Staffordshire villages, talking all the time. Although Colin was fifteen years my senior, the age difference was unimportant to us as we grew closer. In December 1997 I booked another trip to America, and Colin made me promise to write to him every day I was away. Then one day just before I was due to fly out, we were driving back through Stafford when he shyly slipped me a note. In it, he asked me to think about marrying him.

I was astonished to be asked, and almost as surprised to find myself accepting, but I knew that this felt right. I had already spent one uncomfortable Christmas in America, visiting Tommy on Death Row, and I was expecting this visit to be just as difficult – but it would be made even harder by having to leave behind someone who had become so important to me. However, we did write every day, and I was uplifted by knowing that I was loved and missed, and by knowing that Colin cared about what I was doing and thought it worth while. How good God was! He had provided me with an ideal partner and supporter – someone who shared my love of nature, my interests in cricket and music, who had the singing voice of an angel and who cared deeply about helping others. At times, being involved with men on Death Row can be stressful and traumatic. Now I began to find out how helpful it is to have a solid, reliable and loving partner.

We got engaged on Valentine's Day 1998. When Colin's brother Laurie asked him when we planned to marry, he replied, "Some time next year."

"Why?" asked Laurie. "What is there to wait for?"

We realized that there was nothing to hold us back – we both knew our own minds and there was little planning to be done. So we married on 6 June that year, in a very quiet ceremony, with only Laurie and his wife Sheila let into the secret to act as our witnesses. We had a very brief honeymoon in the Lake District, and came home to start our new life together.

To help us make a fresh start Colin and I decided to move to a new home, free of memories. Our requirements were modest, and we soon settled on a small two-bedroomed cottage in the middle of a terrace on the south side of Stafford. As this was a twenty-minute drive from our church, we decided that it was a good time to seek out a new fellowship too. It is hard to take a full part in the life of a church if you don't live locally, and anyway, after twenty years' membership, we realized that it's entirely possible to get into a rut in church.

Was God challenging our complacency in order to move us on in our faith? The older we get, the harder it can be to leave behind familiar forms of worship and step out into the unknown. The more involved we are in church activities, the more likely it is that most of our close friends come from within the church, and moving in those cosy circles of familiarity can make us too comfortable. We knew how much support the church had given us through difficult periods in our lives, and it was hard to consider sacrificing that support system. Yet we knew that

God is always faithful and gracious when we dare to step out in faith, and never abandons us.

We did find a new church – though it came through an unexpected route. For years I had been attending the annual LifeLines conference in London, and that year I slipped a note into the suggestion box which was always placed in the entrance hall. Why, I asked, was the conference always held in London? There were good road and rail links in the provinces, where most of us lived, and there was life north of Watford! It was a big mistake. The organizers were delighted with the idea, and asked me to put it into action: if I wanted a conference outside London, I could organize it.

As a result, I spent a great deal of time hunting for suitable premises – a good-sized hall with kitchen facilities, close to a station – and found that there was actually very little accommodation that fitted both the requirements and the modest budget. In the end I found Church Lane. Originally a Brethren Church known only as The Rooms, it was now a lively Free Evangelical Church, with a reputation for being very active in the local community. It was in the centre of town, close to the station and several cafés and pubs, and the low hiring fee astonished the conference committee, who were used to paying London prices. They told me to book it at once.

Colin and I went along one Friday lunchtime, when the church provided snacks and lunches for shoppers, and met the pastor and some of the church members. They were so warm and welcoming that we started going along to the Sunday services; it was a great change from the Anglican church where we had been worshipping for so long. We had found a new spiritual home – and the LifeLines conference was a great success too.

Change seemed to be in the air. No sooner had we settled down than the young pastor who had welcomed us announced that he was moving on, to work in a Baptist church-planting situation in Somerset. We knew that he would be ideal for the job, but it left the church – and us, as new members – actively seeking a new pastor. Several local candidates were interviewed, but none seemed to be entirely suited to our needs, so the net was cast wider, with advertisements placed in magazines and on the internet. After a year of searching, the right man was found: John, who was well known to the elders and the congregation, and who had often been invited as a visiting preacher. Both John and his wife Linda had great pastoral gifts, and they (and John's mum Connie) came as a wonderful package: God's gift to Church Lane. They were God's gift to Colin and me as well – he knew our spiritual needs and had supplied them as abundantly as ever. We needed a firm, supportive spiritual home if we were to be able to do the work he planned for us. "I have called you friends, because I have disclosed to you everything that I heard from my father. You did not choose me ... I appointed you to go on and bear fruit, fruit that shall last; so that the Father may give you all that you ask in my name" (John 15:15–17).

Meanwhile, the advertisements on the internet had thrown up an unexpected bonus: Ela, a prisoner in Zambia. He came across the church's address and wrote to introduce himself. The church secretary passed his letter on to me and another correspondence was born.

Ela introduced himself as a thirty-year-old Zambian serving the tenth year of a twenty-year sentence:

I have accepted and received Jesus just here in prison as my Lord and Saviour. I realized how dead I was spiritually. My life was empty and meaningless. And I believe a Christian walk is not an easy road. I need someone to encourage and strengthen me ... I need someone to befriend me and correspond with.

He seemed delighted to get a response from me, and wrote back in glowing terms, addressing me as "my beloved mother", which made me feel very old and wise, but didn't really fit in with my preferred self-image!

I warmly greet you in the name of our soon coming king, Jesus Christ. I thank God the Father who gave you the strength and heart to make such a difficult decision and accept me as one of your happy God's family. It gives me great joy and I am always moved in spirit to see God working in the lives of his servants ... I very much longed to hear from you. The words contained in it are precious, uplifting and lovely. Though you are a thousand of miles away, your words and voice in written form have fully brought a lane of inspiration in my life. Thanks dear mum for having read, having heard my voice ... thank you for having introduced me before your prayer group ... you talked of having six pen-friends, that is really great and wonderful in God's eyes. There are simply very few people worldwide who may think/plan to visit or write to prison. But surely if people who are engulfed, entangled are dejected forsaken and isolated who will strengthen them on their prison journey full of hardships?

He described those hardships graphically for me, telling me what he had to endure on a day-to-day basis:

I eat once a day, the meal based on *rishima* from ground maize and beans ... clothes and shoes are a mere dream to me ... toilets are at most times filled with dirty water ... I spend most of my time reading books and on Mondays, Wednesdays and Fridays I teach my fellow inmates junior secondary school science.

Ela recounted the story of how he had become a Christian: in December 1995 a cholera epidemic had raged through the prison population and many prisoners died. He himself was in hospital for twelve days, where he was visited by the hospital chaplain, who worked tirelessly, bringing food and preaching the gospel of God's love to the men. Ela reflected on what he heard, and made the decision to surrender his life to Christ. He wrote in a beautiful, artistic hand, and he was clearly an intelligent, thoughtful and sensitive man, proud of his educational achievements:

> To start with ... I completed Grade 12 in 1991, immediately after completion of school, I committed an offence of aggravated robbery, after joining bad company. Here in prison I laboured vigorously in continuing education and did rewrite history, H/S/biology, commerce and mathematics. Currently I am holder of 7 O levels, the entry grades for university. But I can go no further than this because the prison authorities do not offer education assistance further than this.

It is commonplace for inmates to lose touch with family and friends. Some go for years without seeing loved ones, and the sense of isolation can be overpowering. Ela explained it clearly: "Imagine I don't remember either being visited by relatives or friends for the past ten years I have spent behind bars. Only my Lord our God has been my strength as I traverse through this difficult phase of my life." In such a grim and lonely situation, a letter can be a great blessing:

> Your letter contained very precious words which turned out to be cold water and milk to the very soul of my nature. It found me at an hour I was completely compounded with a lane of loneliness ... I'm filled with great

joy such that my fellow inmates are completely surprised. Your letter has turned out to be my visitor.

On 19 September 2003 he wrote with some good news:

I am always comforted by your love ... and I delight in the wonderful name of our loving Father and God for making it possible for you to write your letter of Tuesday 12th Aug. and Thur 4th Sept. ... It is quite an encourage-ment knowing ... that you will always have me in your loving thoughts ... I am doing it quite well ... and guess what? I was removed from the Maximum Security Prison to a medium security prison just across the road ... on Sept 2nd. Maximum Security is surrounded by very high walls and prisoners are not allowed to move out of prison ... medium security has only wire fencing round it and prisoners go for various work places ... Prisoners are involved in various gangs (working parties) ... please buy me some seeds of various vegetables ... I would like to start a garden of my own, so that I have food supplement.

Ela is now looking forward to the day of his release, and is trying to gather the basic necessities of life, such as blankets and clothing, to equip him for release.

14

Travelling Together

MY **MARRIAGE TO COLIN** had opened a wonderful new chapter in my life. At last I had a companion who shared my interests and concerns, and for the first time in many years I felt loved and supported by someone very special. I was lonely no longer.

Colin made me very happy. In the early days of our marriage he would often ask, "Will you marry me?" as if asking for reassurance that I didn't regret my decision. It made me feel loved and cherished. He was already retired when we married, so he was the one who stayed at home while I went out to work, and he took pride in doing the housework and cooking, though I teased him that he got as much food on the floor as he did on the plates. When I got home I would often come across loving little notes which he left around the house for me to find. I was amused and touched by the irony that I, the inveterate letter-writer, was now on the receiving end of so many hand-written letters!

I am the sort of person who questions everything, so Colin's eternal optimism and quiet, simple faith were a lesson to me – the more so since he was often in pain. Severe arthritis in his hip meant that he found it increasingly difficult to do some things for himself – simple things like putting his socks on, or having a bath or shower unaided. As his condition worsened, he was also unable to drive, and needed wheelchair assistance to get around in town. Our tiny home became like an assault course, cluttered with so many pieces of equipment and aids for the disabled that it was hard for the able-bodied to move about! Having to rely on me for so many things made his illness and incapacity especially trying for him, and he hated to think that he was always making more work for me. Nevertheless he always retained his sense of humour, despite his pain, and he was unfailingly grateful for the help I was only too willing to offer. I often found little notes from him thanking me for my help, or apologizing for being a burden: "Thanks so much for your care and consideration. I do so appreciate it … Thank you for looking after me and putting up with me."

In Colin, I had got myself an incurable romantic. He loved sloppy videos and stories which had happy endings; I preferred true life crime and gritty realism. When there was nothing to watch on television, we would take turns to choose from the local video shop. One weekend I would squirm with embarrassment at the slushy sentimentality of his favourites; the next, Colin would be hiding his eyes in horror and disbelief at the terrible things people do to each other and the inventively gruesome ways they do them. We were not very similar in this respect, but perhaps we complemented each other!

Despite this, he was determined to involve himself in my prison work. He prayed faithfully for all my prison friends, and often added a footnote or two to my letters as I completed them. One day I left a book on the table: it was called simply *Death Row*, and had been written by my friend Shirley about her son Jeff's experiences in prison. Normally I would have expected the title to have warned Colin off, but not this time. By the time I got home he was halfway through it; what's more, once he had finished reading it he started to work his way through my considerable library of books on the subject. He was committed to me, and that meant sharing my commitment to the cause of caring for prisoners. To share in that work, and to play a real and active role, he had realized that he needed to do some homework, and he was getting down to it. How wonderful that God found me such a willing partner.

Colin's first wife, Margaret, had been a reluctant traveller, so they had never ventured far from home. Now Colin enthusiastically embraced the opportunity to go to the USA, and he was looking forward to seeing new places and meeting new people. I was thrilled to have a companion to accompany me on my travels, and I was eager to introduce him to all my American friends, both in and out of prison. However, when his hip got so bad that he needed crutches or a wheelchair to get around, we wondered whether it was wise for him to make the journey. Still, all the arrangements had been made, and we knew that American airlines were able to cope with disabled travellers, so we went ahead.

That Christmas I had been given a book published in the USA: *Chicken Soup for the Prisoner's Soul*. It contained accounts of prison experiences, written by prisoners and by people involved in working with them. At the back was a list of contributors and contact addresses, and as several of these were in the Tennessee area where we would be staying, I dashed off some letters suggesting that we might visit. One of the replies was from Ben, who worked at a 1,250-bed facility for young drug offenders. He invited us to come and look around; he assured me that Colin's mobility problems could be taken care of.

Sure enough, when we arrived, Ben came out to meet us with an English girl called Nicky who was working with him, and they brought with them a shiny, apparently brand-new wheelchair. The chair had been refurbished in the prison's own workshop, one of a batch about to be sent to Poland. Colin was comfortably settled into it, we were given lapel badges to identify us and taken through the inevitable X-ray screening, and our visit began.

Our first call was to the chapel, where we met the chaplain and a large group of staff members. I was horrified to discover that they were expecting me to deliver a lecture on the English penal system and my place in it! I hadn't expected this and was totally unprepared, but there was no way I could refuse when they were making such an effort to welcome us. I muttered a hasty prayer and launched into the best account I could give. I explained that my views were necessarily somewhat subjective, as I was not an expert on policy-making or educational programmes, and my experience was limited to writing to and visiting various institutions, and my friendships with the people in them.

Some of the questions that followed were quite technical, but I did my best, and my audience seemed satisfied. We, of course, had many questions about the system they were implementing in this specialist facility, and they were happy to tell us about it. By a strange coincidence which surprised and delighted me, the rehabilitation scheme used in the prison was also called Life Line. The interesting thing was that many of the staff had been addicted to drugs themselves, so they could understand the problems and challenges presented by the tough rehabilitation programme they were implementing. They also acted as role models for the young men and women in their charge.

Some aspects of this unusual prison seemed extremely strange to our British eyes. One was the "inmate council". At four in the afternoon, the men gathered in the large central hall, and sat in rows as if in a courtroom. One by one, inmates with a complaint against another prisoner came forward and made their case to the audience. The offender could make a brief response by way of mitigation or explanation, and the "jury" of onlookers would then suggest a suitable punishment, such as the withdrawal of a privilege for twenty-four hours. All the punishments were minor, but apparently the system worked well and had the respect of the inmates.

An even more bizarre ritual followed. At the end of the council, all the men formed a large circle round the perimeter of the hall, and linked up with hands on each other's shoulders. Then they began a chant, about 300 words long. It had been written by the inmates themselves and they had all learned it by heart and used it as a daily mantra to remind themselves of their situation and their aims.

Besides the 250 men in Ben's unit, there were eighty women in a separate unit next door. We looked around one dormitory for twelve women: it was neat and bright, with the bunk beds tidily made. Colin told the women it reminded him of his days in the RAF.

"Every day," he said, "the NCO would inspect our billet, wearing a pair of white gloves. He checked the tops of beds and cupboards and woe betide you if those gloves showed any sign of dust! Once a week there was a full inspection, when all our kit had to be laid out for scrutiny by the duty officer. We used to put pads on our feet and skid around polishing the floor – it had to be so shiny you could see your face in it."

The girls were giggling. "Please don't give them any more ideas for things they can make us do!" they said.

When we left we were given a booklet about the substance abuse treatment programme. Statistics indicated that almost 70 per cent of felonies in the USA were directly or indirectly linked with drugs, and from 1980 to 1992 the number of people jailed for drug crimes almost tripled. The costs to society were evident. The sponsors of the rehabilitation programme were quick to point out its effectiveness: for every dollar spent on drug treatment programmes, the taxpayer enjoyed a return of $4 in the reduction of drug-crime-related costs.

The booklet also included the personal testimonies of men who had passed through the programme, and they made fascinating reading. The intensive, six-month treatment programme aimed to make drug abusers confront their problems, change their attitudes and modify their behaviour.

"Before being incarcerated, I had turned to drugs for a solution to all the problems in my life. In reality, my idea of a solution became my biggest problem ... I now realize that I can't deny my problems, and I am ultimately responsible for my actions."

Another man said, "Life Line has taught me to control my thoughts, like when a problem in my life occurs, an immediate positive solution is required. I accept the things I cannot change. Life is 10 per cent of what happens to me and 90 per cent of how I react to it."

There was a strong spiritual element present throughout the programme, and many of the staff and inmates we met were Christians. During our visit we were free to wander around wherever we wished, and able to talk freely with anyone we met. Several times we gathered a small group around us, and sat in a quiet corner talking to them, asking about their experiences and their hopes for the future. On each occasion, when they heard that we were Christians from England, the inmates invited us to pray with them, blessing us and being blessed by the fellowship and the prayer.

One man called Charles wrote in the testimony booklet: "The third phase of Life Line really taught me how to live on life's terms. Learning the 12-step program and developing the spirituality in my life taught me how to have a more responsible and positive way of living."

It was notable that after graduating from the rehabilitation programme, inmates remained in the scheme for some months, helping others to complete the training. On their release they also received after-care in the community, which offered another safeguard against relapsing into old ways and old temptations. "My alcohol abuse and criminal behaviour seem to go hand in hand. There's been many times when I've tried to turn around and leave this lifestyle behind, but I couldn't." Another man added: "I have been in and out of institutions for the last 20 years of my life ... I feel better today than I've ever felt ... I'm in prison, but I feel free."

There could be no better recommendation for the scheme than that comment, we felt. Drug addiction is a prison of its own, and by releasing people from their addiction we are truly setting them free to make their own choices and live a better, more law-abiding life. It is clearly worth while to support such activities as this, and on this visit we were glad to meet so many people who shared our concern for the rehabilitation of offenders.

My friend Jacqueline invited us to attend a house group with her, at the large city church where she was a member. It was a warm, lively place, and we immediately felt at home. We were delighted to learn that 300 church members were regularly involved with prison work – an impressive number, and an unusual church. Harmon, who is a Rhodes scholar and teacher of Prison Ministry at the School of Divinity at Vanderbilt University, told us of some visits he was making to local Methodist groups.

"They are good and generous folk," he said. "If you ask them to dip into their pockets and give to the work, they do so willingly and freely. But if you suggest to them that they visit a real person behind bars, and get personally involved, they balk at the idea and don't want to know. It's a step too far."

This reflected my own experience. Some of my

Christian friends were very interested to hear my stories, and were glad to know that the work was going on, but try as I might, I couldn't entice them to become part of it.

Colin, however, was more than willing to join me in caring for prisoners. He added his own little messages to my letters, and the prisoners in turn included him in their replies. One day he sent Roberto a description of the work we had been doing in our tiny garden. In spite of its small size we had managed to fill it with colour, and we both loved working on it together. In the warmer months we spent as much time as possible outside, tending the plants and shrubs and growing our own vegetables. Roberto wrote back enthusiastically.

> Colin thanks for keeping me in mind, I always think of my good friends too, and keep asking God to keep each one of you well. My Grand Mother always told me that you need a good kind hand to plant and fix things, your cottage is looking good and that show how much love you and Penny are putting in it each time you too work in and around it.

When he told José how much he liked watching birds, José (who was a talented artist) did some drawings specially for him, showing various native American species. I teased poor José about it in my next letter, pointing out that I had been his pen-friend much longer than Colin, yet he was the one that was blessed with the art work. Knowing that he enjoyed a joke, I said that I would put a curse on him so that his hair would fall out and terrible things would happen to his manhood. Predictably, another drawing followed, this time addressed to me, with the comment: "Penny I have to tell you your curse it is working, my hair is gone south and I have had no use for my genitals for years." Colin was surprised (as I had been when I first made contact with prisoners) how much fun and humour there was in our relationships.

The men were also eager to give advice on any of our various domestic troubles, be they physical, emotional or spiritual. Colin received many suggestions for remedies to relieve his painful arthritis – from exercise routines to patent medicines, including dubious potions and nostrums more associated with witch doctors than twenty-first century pharmacology. They were always very supportive, and I especially appreciated the opportunity to talk to impartial "outsiders", as I had few family members of my own to consult. They welcomed the chance to help: their opinions counted for very little in the wider world, written off by society as they were. Showing them respect by asking their opinions brought us love and respect in turn from them.

Our marriage had led to some tensions among the six children Colin and I had between us from our previous marriages, and my youngest daughter Alison was particularly difficult. Roberto was concerned:

> Tell me have you talked to your youngest daughter yet? I pray that your relationship with her be as it suppose to be between a mother and a daughter. I know that you will find a way to reach her because she is in your heart is you can find the patience for those like me that you do not know but yet bless our lives with your time and love then I can only wonder all that you would do for your little girl … don't give up my friend the sun will shine on your wishes one day.

Colin was discovering, as I had, that prison relationships didn't just work in one direction. We might be very willing to give our time and friendship freely – but it was repaid many times over with a generosity of spirit that frequently surprised us.

15

Prison Life

LIKE ME, COLIN FOUND THE PRISON an intimidating environment. It was strange to be introducing him to so many new experiences, and I realized that over the years I had become an old hand at managing the bureaucracy of visitor permits and body searches, so that I hardly thought about them. However, I never became accustomed to the prison atmosphere, nor to the constant awareness that Unit Two was there for one purpose only – to hold men who were awaiting their death.

Tennessee is one of the southern states which tend to have an Old Testament attitude to law and order and crime and punishment. Their thinking runs along the lines of "an eye for an eye, and a tooth for a tooth", and "if you do the crime, you do the time". Their legislators and law enforcement agencies take a tough stance, and the possibility of redemption and forgiveness seems to be alien to their way of thinking. I don't know how they square this with their profession of Christian belief, but they seem to place the emphasis entirely on judgement rather than on mercy, and that includes reliance on the death penalty as a form of punishment.

Some people believe that Christians should not work in a place where killing is sanctioned by the state; by doing so, they may be thought to be condoning the act. Others think that Christians should be involved in every aspect of life, and try to influence things for good. I hadn't given either viewpoint much thought until I met Nancy. Small and dumpy, with greying hair and a ready smile, she worked mainly at the front desk in reception, where her bright and cheerful personality made an impression on me; we liked each other right away. Unlike the other prison officers, who could be morose and surly with visitors, Nancy was a chatterbox, and soon got into conversation with me; she was interested in the curious circumstances which brought me to visit the prison.

Nancy was a Christian of strong convictions, and she was delighted to meet another Christian from England, who believed she had a role in ministering to prisoners. She usually gave me only a cursory, token frisking, and never bothered to make me take my shoes off for inspection. I sensed a deep loneliness in her, and I knew she looked forward to our snatched conversations when she was on duty. At first she said that she would love it if I would write to her, too, from England, but after talking it over with her husband, she withdrew her request. Apparently prison rules forbade her to fraternize with the friends of inmates, and she could have lost her job. I sent her a couple of notes from England, but told her not to reply; instead, she sometimes managed to send me messages from time to time when some of my English LifeLiner friends were visiting. I would get a phone call when they returned: "Nancy says Hi, and she hopes you're doing good. She sends her love."

Nancy was sympathetic about Colin's arthritis, and interested to know when he was hoping to have his hip replacement operation. The joke was that for some reason Colin always sets off the alarms when he walks through the screening equipment at airports, and has to be exhaustively searched for whatever obscure metal item he has secreted about his person (once it was a radiator bleeding key in his pocket!) which is causing the problem.

The last time it had been metal inserts in the soles of his shoes, which were only revealed by the X-ray machine.

"We'll never be allowed into the country again," I said, "once Colin has a hip full of metal." I was worried about the prison scanning machines too.

"Oh, no, you'll be fine," Nancy reassured us. "When I broke my foot the surgeon put a metal plate in it, and I thought when I got back to work I'd be pulled up feet-first by the magnets, and left hanging upside down! Fortunately surgical steel doesn't set off the alarm."

The prison had a high turnover of staff, as the job involved long hours of boring work for very low pay, but Nancy always seemed to be cheerful. We enjoyed her company, and she didn't seem to share the local opinion of what prisoners deserved.

I'm sure that the general public's attitude to crime – that jails are for punishment, not rehabilitation – is responsible for the harsh conditions in the prisons. The surroundings are uniformly stark and bland: everything is cold, clinical and colourless, as if sensory deprivation were part of the punishment. Even the public areas are bare, with the minimum of clutter and no decoration. It's a way of managing a situation where the men far outnumber the prison staff: design out all humanity and all uncertainty. Don't give them any places to hide; keep all areas clear, in case the staff have to "rush" someone; make sure there is nothing around that can be fashioned into a weapon. Everyone in prison has a number, because by reducing people to impersonal case numbers, it is more acceptable to treat them less than humanely, as if these individuals were no more than the sum of their crimes.

I always did my best to bring normal human warmth into this impersonal set-up. When we were visiting Tommy we naturally got to know many of the other prisoners in the visiting area, and Michael, the unit's barber, was a well-known figure. He was teased a lot because he was very fond of my middle daughter, Hilary, and always looked out for her when I was visiting. On one occasion Michael wasn't in the main visiting area, and when I finally spotted him he was being placed in a side room by the guard. He waved cheerily to me through the window, but the guard turned the key on him and prevented me from entering. The stout metal door had a wide slot in it; it was made like this so that less trustworthy inmates could be handled safely by a single officer. When he was to be moved from the room, the man had to back up to the door and place his hands behind him through the slot; then the guard could safely put handcuffs on him before unlocking the door and returning him to his cell. I was able to use this slot: I pushed my hands through and offered them to Michael, who clasped them eagerly. It's easy to forget the importance of physical contact in such a sterile environment; the men hated being confined to the safe rooms during visiting time. Most of them would rather lose their radios – an important link with the out-side world – than be denied the chance to hug and hold a loved one.

Maximum security prisons often have extended peri-ods of "lockdown" – usually if there is a security scare, an escape attempt or a killing. During this time, no visitors are allowed in, and the men spend their time locked in their cells. Such lengthy enforced sabbaticals mean that the men are thrown back on whatever resources they have to entertain themselves. Rob wrote to me of one such episode:

Since the beginning of April we have been on a complete lockdown without the access to receive visit or anything else after an inmate tried to kill an officer and there is no telling how long we will remain on lockdown. I guess I will have to postpone my birthday! We usually spend one third of the year [like this] but it looks like this year it would be for the whole year.

The unwelcome spell of confinement finally came to an end, and he wrote to tell us of the simple pleasure of being allowed outside: "I have a little sun burned yesterday morning, finally I made it outside of my cell, it felt good to walked around the yard for a while and inhaled some fresh air."

Yet another period of lockdown followed:

The post is running better now, the writing materials was not confiscated, the problem is that since May 17th we have been in a complete lockdown and most of us run out of something by now, I am out of stamps a while back but my sister sent me some and that's why I am able to answer your letter now. We are still on lockdown but we are not in a state of emergency, maybe by the end of the month we will be able to go to the store (prison commissary) and get what we usually need.

The potential for violence in all prisons was brought home to me by Rob when he was transferred from the cell he shared with José in Pelican Bay to a different jail in California. Moving to a new institution is a major upheaval in many ways. Not only do you lose contact with people you have come to trust, of whom there are precious few, but you have to learn a new "pecking order" and establish yourself with a group of men to whom you are an unknown and therefore dangerous quantity. It can be a tough time, learning which men to avoid, which to respect, which to trust, and which are likely to cause trouble. There are new rules and routines, new prison personnel, new surroundings, new pressures. Rob's personal life was in turmoil anyway, after the death of his brother, and he found the move a trial. He wrote to tell me of his anguish:

> My friend I try to face my hard time with pride and dignity. I have learn to be strong but this year started without my little brother and now for a whole week now I have been watching the face of my people after the 7.6 earthquake that my country took ... what hurts me more its unable to do something, thanks God my loved ones are OK ... my life has not been easy but I still have a lot, I have a heart full of hope, a lot of good friends ... and a good wife, how can I complain?

Shortly after the move he found himself in fear of his life. "My dear friend I am facing one of the worse problems a man can face in prison, I have been accused by the inmates of being a snitch ... God knows how this is going to end." Even Rob's handwriting as he wrote these words was not his usual careful, neat script. I could sense the panic in this message, but apart from praying for the situation I was powerless to help. Apparently it was a case of mistaken identity, and was typical of the way wrong information can cause a perilous situation to arise in the heightened tension of the prison. Rob had been involved in two fights over an incident which took place at a prison he had never even been inside. Prisoners don't stop to check facts or take an objective look at things: the mere rumour of being a "snitch" can get a man killed.

It isn't easy to know what to write to someone facing such a grave situation, but I assured Rob of our prayers at all times, and I heard that the prison staff were aware of what was going on, so I hoped they would look out for him. We were immensely relieved when his next letter came:

Penny the problem I was facing at the beginning of the year are now becoming a faint memory now I am surround by good friends and getting stronger every day, not just in body but in mind. Thank you and Colin for remembering me in your prayers, during those times of trouble I got closer to God.

Meanwhile there was still his appeal to keep up his hopes. I had written to José, back in Pelican Bay, telling him that the Los Angeles Police Department was under investigation for corrupt practices, and many cases they had prosecuted were being re-examined. Some sentences had already been overturned on the grounds of malpractice. José was delighted:

Good news are the comment you said, or made about Roberto's case going back to court in his appeal, and since his case comes from Rampart Station, which is the one in investigation for corruption, maybe his case is among those that were tainted with the wrong-doing of these officer, depending on the year Roberto was arrested. So he might be lucky; you know Penny I was apprehended by the same police station so long ago.

Other problems also contribute to the misery of incarceration: for instance, the medical care is usually inadequate. Taxpayers don't see why they should pay for felons to get treatment. When Jeff died of a heart attack while in prison, we wondered whether he might have survived had he received better medical attention. Tommy told me that he had once requested an urgent dental appointment when he had raging toothache; the prison nurse gave him Tylenol, an over-the-counter painkiller which was totally inadequate to control the pain. After waiting three months without seeing a dentist, he was desperate. He managed to get hold of some pliers and somehow pulled out the tooth himself – leaving behind a splinter of tooth embedded in his jaw, which later flared up and caused yet more pain.

It was always worrying when we heard that any of our friends were ill. Farid, who had a job cleaning the unit, was badly burned when a bottle of bleach exploded. Initially he was blinded, and though he later regained some sight in one eye, he never fully recovered. José, too, had worries about his health: he had stomach pains and was eventually sent for some tests. "I have good news about my health, the ultrasound test came back normal, which means no cancer: what of relief really though the blood test showed that my cholesterol level is slightly above the normal level."

He was also worried about his mother, who was in hospital for a liver problem. As she was a Jehovah's Witness (a faith which rejects the possibility of blood transfusions) he was specially concerned about what treatment she might need.

> As for my health it is fine and thankfully with the medications, exercises and some sacrifices from my meals to avoid any heart problems, everything is going well and I'm still waiting for the results of my stomach X-rays, to find out if I have an ulcer. I guess no news is good news, as for my mother, she is doing well at the moment.

Several letters later he wrote that he had received a surprise visit

> ... from my mum and sister along with a friend after twelve years, I was bursting with happiness and though it was only two hours in a booth behind a glass window, we enjoyed our time together; my mother has change so much but my sister is still the same.

Life in prison is an emotional roller-coaster: in an atmosphere where a careless or hasty word can trigger an explo-
sion of violence and result in a killing, men and women
live in a constant state of tension. Their hopes can be
raised by the possibility of an appeal hearing or a parole
board, and dashed again. Things which we on the outside
take for granted, like a telephone call to a loved one, are
major events to them. Letters are welcome diversions, and
the knowledge that someone is interested in their fate
makes a huge difference to them.

> Remember that it is a pleasure to hear from you and
> answer your letters which are full of life and joy. Thank
> you very much for lighten my cloudy day – take care of
> yourself, give my regards to Colin and to all your friends
> and love ones, may God bless you always, sincerely your
> friend, Roberto.

Wanting to repay us in whatever way he could, Rob kept
asking for photos of the two of us, so that he could make
a drawing from them:

> Try to send me some pictures of you and Colin but if you
> can, send them 8 x 10 to make it easier for me to do a por-
> trait … I would like to do something very nice for you, to
> show you how much I appreciated your friendship. I
> hope to hear from you soon, on the meantime take good
> care of yourself and may God bless you always.

Rob often used the lockdown time to perfect his art work:
" … luckily for me I use this time … for my drawings. I
want to do something for you … that you like, would you
help me out there and give me an idea?" We responded by
sending a snapshot of the two of us, which provoked a wry
comment from Rob:

Penny thank you for the photo, is not good enough to surprise you with a portrait, but it is clear enough to see you and Colin. Tell Colin not to wear the clothes he has on in the photo if he comes to California, otherwise the authorities may think that he just got out of jail.

Both José and Rob loved to draw – a skill which Rob had shared with José when they shared their cell in Pelican Bay.

Thanks for sending my note to José, the next time you write to him pull his ears for me. Tell him I was hoping to heard from him through you ... I pray to God every day keep on pushing him to keep up with his drawings, I started as soon as I came out of the hole, tell him that I still remember when he told me that he did not had the hand to draw, but with time and patience everything is possible.

However, it was never easy for the men to find the materials they needed. I tried to help when I could, but the maze of regulations often defeated me. Prisoners were allowed to receive photographs (provided they were not Polaroids), stamps, books (if they came direct from the bookseller) and cassette tapes (as long as they were the transparent sort, and thus useless for smuggling drugs). However, at times many of these allowances were revoked, and for some reason stamps and tapes were no longer permissible. In theory, José could receive paper: "As for what I can get for artwork, actually not a thing, common blank paper, that's it, although if you want to help me perhaps when you come to the States, you can send me writing paper, a few (10) embossed envelopes, and a few sheets of blank paper."

However, I found the reality somewhat different. A stout brown A4 envelope containing a variety of pastel-coloured paper and a pack of coloured pencils was inexplicably returned to me several weeks later. A sticky label on the front informed me that it was regarded as "contraband" and contained "an unidentified substance". Quite what that was, I never worked out. I couldn't help thinking that the prison authorities deliberately restricted the men's access to anything that might encourage their creativity or make their limited lives more tolerable.

Despite all these obstacles, José managed to shower us with glorious examples of his unique ability. Colin, Alison, Hilary and I all received cards for our birthdays; he took any excuse for a card – Valentine's Day, Mother's Day, Christmas – to use his talent as a way to thank us.

> My, my, it's so good to hear from you dear friend, your lovely letter brought a smile to my face. You know something, I was missing you already, that's how much your letters means to me ... As you can see I'm sending you a drawing, I made it a while back ... since the one I'm doing for you for Hallowe'en is not finish ... so I hope you like it anyways, also by now those drawing I sent for Alison, Hils birthday should got there, I wish they like them.

Roberto, too, was busy with card-making: "My friend, sorry for not writting sooner but I did something for Mother's Day which I thought that it was going to be easy, but it end up taking more than a month to do it and working real hard on it daily."

Inmates in America's prisons can receive money, paid into their trust accounts via a money order – they are not allowed "green" money, meaning notes or cash. The trust money may be used to purchase stamps, soft drinks or toiletries, or to pay for telephone calls. I did sometimes send small amounts of money to my friends, but I wasn't able to offer much in the way of financial assistance, living as I did on a low income and a necessarily tight budget.

Before I knew the rules about bank notes, I had sent some dollar bills inside a letter. They had been removed by the time my friend received the letter, and we concluded that someone in the prison mailroom had pocketed them. I learned my lesson the hard way, and decided to send only postage stamps from then on. I had several friends to support, and I was anxious not to favour one over another. I was a pen-friend, and pen-friendship was really all I had to offer.

The one thing I could do was to write letters – not only to my friends, but often on their behalf. When you have a pen-friend in prison, much of the conversation is concerned with court appearances and appeals, and sometimes friends ask you to read briefs or court dockets. I was often asked to write to prison governors and parole boards on behalf of friends, and act as a character witness when they came up before the authorities. José wrote to me:

> How are you doing my good friend? ... I'm hoping this little letter find you and your family in God's hands. As for me very happy! ... Remember I was waiting for the Review Board approval to be transfer and release from the SHU [Secure Housing Unit]; well I got it, so within two months I'll be out of here. You know Penny, my parole board is coming up on Dec 18th, so I need you to write me a letter of support again ... I will appreciate your help ... that's why I'm going through all these obstacles from the courts, hoping I catch a good judge, get a break, to force this institution to reclassify me and release me to another prison where I can go to school and learn a trade.

He was delighted when he heard about his transfer:

> I have good news in regard of my release from the SHU. Yesterday, in the late afternoon, I was called to appear in

front of the DRB and they approved me for the program
I had mentioned and chances are I get to see David [a previous cell-mate, transferred a year earlier] because I'm
going to be sent to the same institution ... I'll be getting
out of here within two months, and a lot closer to Los
Angeles, so my mum might get to see me soon ... perhaps
I'll be having Christmas in a better environment than
here.

"A better environment" was often the best these men
could hope for. Most of them accepted that for all their
hopes of appeal hearings and parole boards, they would
be spending the foreseeable future locked up within the
dreary prison regime. For those on Death Row, like
Tommy, this was the best possibility – the alternative was
unthinkable. How could anyone cope with such a situation?

I was talking one day with my friend Maria, a retired
nurse tutor who was also staying at the guest house. She
described how her friend Michael bade her goodbye at the
end of a visit. He stood around in the entrance hall, by the
officer's desk, chatting to the guard on duty and the other
men who had received a visitor. He switched his attention
away from her in a somewhat brusque manner as she left
the building, not lingering by the glass doorway to wave
her up the walkway. It was as if he was mentally washing
his hands of Maria, the representative of the outside
world. I had noticed similar conduct among my friends:
as soon as you prepared to leave, they switched off.

I made a mental note to watch how the inmates spoke
and interacted among themselves, and realized that they
appeared to have a private understanding among themselves, a kind of prison-speak code, which excluded the
likes of us. The shared experience included the guards,
though not those of us on the outside – it was as though

both sets of people, captive and captors, were in the same boat, both living in the same strange, twilight world, far removed from normal life. We few visitors were allowed limited access, but we could never understand the reality of that world, with its own rules and conditions. The environment was certainly a hostile one, but the prisoners had adapted to it, and evolved strategies for coping; survival mechanisms which required that we others were shut out as soon as we approached the exit which was forbidden to them. We were transient, and though they enjoyed our visits, they blanked us out as soon as we left, shutting off the disturbance so that they could settle back into their normal state.

16

Debating the Death Penalty

FOR ALL MY GROWING FAMILIARITY with the prison environment, and my deepening friendships with prisoners, one issue still weighed heavily on my mind: the ongoing debate about the death penalty. Although the penalty has not been legal in the UK for forty years, from time to time the question is raised in the media – usually in response to some particularly unpleasant crime – and the arguments are rehearsed again. In the USA, where it is still practised, it is still discussed regularly, especially among my LifeLiner colleagues who are actively campaigning for its abolition.

I have always felt sure that many people support capital punishment through ignorance. Because the event takes place behind closed doors, often in the early hours of the morning, and far away from the public gaze, people are unaware of the horror of execution. They are cushioned from the fact that by giving the action their support, they are themselves engaged in the killing process. I remember some time ago, when a man named Michael Fay had been sentenced by the Singapore courts to caning. There were hundreds of outraged letters in the press, condemning his beating as "inhumane". Yet many of the same people had no qualms about killing someone in the electric chair or by lethal injection.

Those in favour of capital punishment have several standard arguments, but in my opinion only one really stands up to scrutiny: that of prevention. That is, preventing that particular offender from ever committing another crime. Obviously, a dead criminal will never offend again.

The parallel argument is deterrence: that executing some criminals will deter others from committing similar crimes. This is far from certain. It is the fear of crime (which is usually out of all proportion to its actual prevalence) which makes the public demand severe penalties to halt its escalation. State execution is seen as one way to deter criminals from offending – yet some states which implement the death penalty have higher rates of serious crime, notably murder, than those which do not. It is possible that state-sanctioned killing sends out the opposite signal: that killing is acceptable, that human life is cheap, and murder does provide an acceptable answer to a problem. The death penalty brutalizes society.

It is hard to prove whether the death penalty works as a deterrent. It is true that there is far less serious crime in those countries such as Singapore which almost always carry out death sentences; this suggests that it does deter, but only where execution is an absolute certainty. However, in most countries the number of people actually executed each year (compared with the number sentenced to death) is usually a very small proportion. On the whole, in the US, statistics indicate that the death penalty either makes no difference to the number of murders, or actually causes them to increase.

Another argument is cost: some people feel that the state should spend its limited resources on supporting the vulnerable members of society – the elderly, the young and the sick – rather than on the expensive incarceration of felons. Better, they say, to execute criminals than lock them up for life, at enormous financial cost to society. Of course, it isn't that simple. Justice and human rights demand that the full legal process is made available before the final decision for the death penalty is taken, and consequently capital cases have enhanced procedural and evidence requirements, and a mandatory appeals procedure – both costly and time-consuming. A death penalty case costs far more than a normal trial and life imprisonment.

A major element in the demand for capital punishment is revenge. This is only to be expected: when a loved one is brutally murdered, it's understandable that people want to hit out in rage and sorrow. They want retribution – they want the criminal to suffer in proportion to the offence. However, it seems unlikely that achieving such revenge actually benefits the bereaved. Living under a cloud of vengeful thoughts merely stifles the spirit and stunts the personality. Four notable cases spring to mind.

Jane Ewart-Biggs's husband was killed by a car bomb planted by the IRA; Gordon Wilson's daughter was killed at a Remembrance Day cenotaph service at Enniskillen in Northern Ireland; Terry Waite, the envoy of the Archbishop of Canterbury, was held captive in Beirut while himself on a mission to secure the release of other hostages; Jill Saward was the victim of a horrific rape at the vicarage in Ealing, London, where her father was the Anglican priest. What all these people have in common is their steadfast refusal to demand revenge. All of them spoke of forgiving their aggressors; they grew through their anger and grief and emerged as truly whole, inspirational people. They are universally respected and admired. Those who can never get beyond their hatred are permanently imprisoned within themselves by their desire for vengeance.

Dr Martin Luther King spoke of the degenerative nature of violence:

The ultimate weakness of violence is that it is a descending spiral, begetting the very thing it seeks to destroy. Instead of diminishing evil, it multiplies it. Through violence, you murder the liar, but you cannot murder the lie, nor establish the truth. Through violence, you murder the hater but you do not murder hate. In fact, violence merely increases hate – returning violence for violence multiplies violence, adding deeper darkness to a night already devoid of stars. Darkness cannot drive out darkness; only light can do that. Hate cannot drive out hate; only love can do that.

Logic leads one to the inevitable conclusion: if premeditated killing is wrong, then state-sanctioned killing is also wrong.

My own original objection to the death penalty was the fact that there had been many well-known miscarriages of justice over the years, and too many innocent people had paid the ultimate price for crimes they didn't commit. Criminal proceedings are fallible – and in the US, where costs are high, lack of finance means that many defendants are represented by court-appointed lawyers who have little experience. All criminal trials may involve mistakes, but in the case of the death penalty there is no possibility of those mistakes being corrected.

Some people argue that the long-drawn-out appeal procedure reduces the possibility of such errors, but this in itself is a form of cruelty. To put a man to death years, maybe decades after the crime for which he received the sentence, is to subject him to years of fear and torment, far worse than simple imprisonment. Such torture is wrong: some executions are botched and the executed suffer unimaginable pain, but even those who die instantly have suffered mental torture leading up to the execution.

Most of all, the death penalty denies the possibility of redemption. My opposition to capital punishment was

reinforced once I had personal interactions with the convicted killers and knew them not as names on legal dockets, but as flesh-and-blood human beings. The person who
is finally dispatched is often totally different from the one
who committed the original crime. Many men change
beyond recognition during their long incarceration. They
have time – lots of it – to reflect on their lives. They come
to terms with who and what they were, and make deci-
sions not to repeat past mistakes. They yearn for a second
chance (a luxury which they acknowledge they have
denied to their victims). They hope some day to prove
their change of heart.

I asked Tommy about this once, and he told me about
the attitudes which he believed had led him into trouble.

> I can attribute most of my problems to my youthful
> behavior at the time as well. Sure I was an adult but I was
> always looking to cut corners in making a living instead
> of just plain hard work. I didn't know the value of a dol-
> lar because I made it so easily at times. I did things that I
> knew were wrong beforehand and with a mind set cut out
> a path without fear of danger or consequence.

Errol put forward a similar explanation of what had
landed him behind bars: "I know you came from a good
home, just as I did, but I chose my way of doing things.
Drugs, money, fast cars and scandalous women (if you
know what I'm saying)."

I was convinced that Tommy had learned a salutary lesson from his long prison stretch:

> There is a very big difference with us and comes in the old
> adage of "with age comes wisdom". I've grown a lot men-
> tally in the last twelve years and I'm not the same person
> I was then ... I no longer subscribe to the "easy come,
> easy go" theory ... I can no longer afford to take things

for granted as I once did, time is too precious to waste now. Who was quoted as saying "I recognize the enemy and it's me".

The more men I met on the Row, and the more stories I read of people in their situation, the more reassured I was that they would be most unlikely to repeat the aberrant behaviour patterns which had brought them here. One wrote:

> I have no reason to return to my past lifestyle after surviving this ugly nightmare for so long. I'm older now and my attitude has changed significantly. I'm much more mellow and subdued and more than ready to settle into a peaceful co-existence. I've had my fill of living on the edge quite frankly but I must add in my defence how these things occurred in my younger years and at a time when I thought I knew all the answers to life.

Most touching for me was an incident when I was staying at the Reconciliation guest house. The office needed another bookcase, and Meg, who worked there, was asked to go and buy one. She invited me to go along, and we went to the shop and chose a suitable flat-pack. Kaki and Jaqueline, who ran the office, had already signed an open cheque for her, so she filled in the amount and handed it to the cashier. As we made our way to the car, lugging our purchase between us, she confided how much pleasure it had given her to fill out that cheque. She was out of prison after serving an eight-year sentence for cheque fraud, and it meant everything to her to be trusted by the people at Reconciliation.

"A leopard doesn't change its spots" – if I had a £5 note for every time I've heard that said, I could charter my own private jet to fly to America. In this case we aren't talking about external marking, but men's hearts, which can and do change. Think of St Paul. As Saul, he was among the fiercest opponents of Christianity: "So they stoned Stephen ... and Saul was among those who approved his murder" (Acts 7:59; 8:1).

> You have heard what my manner of life was when I was still a practising Jew: how savagely I persecuted the church of God, and tried to destroy it ... But then in his good pleasure God, who had set me apart from birth and called me through his grace, chose to reveal his Son to me and through me, in order that I may proclaim him to the Gentiles. (Galatians 1:13, 15–16)

What about the criminal who was crucified alongside Jesus and who acknowledged his kingship with his final breath? "And he said, 'Jesus, remember me when you come to your throne.' He answered, 'I tell you this: today you shall be with me in Paradise'" (Luke 23:42–43).

Then there is the guard who had charge of Paul and his companions in prison, and who was converted, along with his family, after the earthquake.

> The jailer woke up to see the prison doors wide open, and assuming that the prisoners had escaped, drew his sword, intending to kill himself. But Paul shouted, "Do yourself no harm; we are all here." The jailer called for lights, rushed in and threw himself down before Paul and Silas, trembling with fear. He then escorted them out and said, "Masters, what must I do to be saved?" They said, "Put your trust in the Lord Jesus, and you will be saved." (Acts 16:27–31)

There are many such examples of men and women having a change of heart, and of the dramatic difference it subsequently made to their lives. The very act of becoming a Christian is just that: repentance, an about-turn, a radical, life-changing decision to follow in Jesus' footsteps. As the baptismal promises say, "I turn to Christ. I repent of my sins. I renounce evil." We have to believe in the power of God's redemptive love, or we are all damned. As Christians, it is our commission to give others the chance to make that change, and we are urged never to give up on it. "Therefore, my beloved brothers, stand firm and immovable, and work for the Lord always, work without limit, since you know that in the Lord your labour cannot be lost" (1 Corinthians 15:58).

It's ironic that the prison authorities in America style themselves as the "Department of Correction", when correcting behaviour plays no part in their thinking or their remit. At times of execution, the Department of Extinction might be more appropriate. Yet so many of the men I knew had "corrected" themselves over time. Tommy, José and Roberto had all done some serious self-examination, and I knew of many others, but all too few would ever be given the chance to prove it. Yet surely rehabilitation could be made to work, if only we treated offenders as individuals, instead of lumping them all together. Some of them certainly do have serious personality disorders, and need to be locked away securely, perhaps for ever, but most are not like that. Many of these men found themselves in a situation which escalated out of control, and which produced an impulsive response which they later regretted. With proper training and useful jobs of work inside the prison system, and actual rather than theoretical support structures on the outside when they are released, many could be resocialized and become productive citizens.

How could such systems be created? We need to embark on extensive research into criminality. It is said that one measure of a civilized society is how it treats its most vulnerable members: the poor, the young, the sick and the elderly. Should we include in this list the criminal element

– the least desirable section of the community? If we are to have any hope of stemming the rising tide of crime, or of dealing adequately with offenders when they are imprisoned, we need to try to discover what makes people embark on a life of crime. We must consult them, and make use of their unique insight. Only when we appreciate and understand their perspective can we hope to formulate effective procedures successfully enough to deter them from crime, or rehabilitate them when they do offend.

Both the British and American justice systems are failing: it fails the victims, who feel forgotten, side-lined and unheard, and who rarely think that the punishment fits the crime. It also fails the offenders, who generally reoffend, and whose attitudes become increasingly hardened and antisocial. As a result, whole communities are unhappy, frustrated and living in fear of crime. We need to investigate the underlying causes of crime and put in place properly thought-out measures to alleviate them. This may be costly, but in the long term not as costly as the alternative of leaving things as they are and seeing crimes of violence increase. We need to tackle the social causes, homelessness and unemployment, and be prepared to rethink our attitude to drugs, perhaps the greatest modern menace.

Ex-offenders must be involved in this policy-making process. They, after all, know what makes youngsters turn into offenders, and what can be done to stop the trend. They are a source of important information, as yet largely untapped. Most important, it is up to Christians to seek the one lost sheep and consider Jesus' mercy to the dying thief, as a testimony of grace to the most despised among us. The best insurance we have against recidivist behaviour is for people of faith to get alongside men and women in our penal institutions and embrace them as fellow-sinners, loved by God.

Tommy showed me how much change is possible for an offender. On one occasion we had a discussion about the country's moral decline. I suggested that outside influences such as drug and alcohol abuse, together with violence on TV and video, were at least partly to blame for youngsters becoming desensitized to the feelings of others. I argued that young people were deprived of their innocence by society's distorted attitudes to sex, and its devaluing of all humanity's finer instincts. I was sure that the squalid stories that the media love to dwell on could only have a bad effect on developing young minds. "Perverse and crooked generation whose faults have proved you no children of his, is this how you repay the Lord, you brutish and stupid people?" (Deuteronomy 32:5–6).

Tommy listened attentively. He didn't disagree, but he insisted that adults were entirely responsible for their own actions. He cited as an example two young men looking at a sexually explicit magazine: one put it aside and went back to work; the other went out and raped a young woman. Each had a choice about how he reacted to the stimulus. As for the rapist, Tommy said, "No one made him do that. No one held a gun to his head."

I found Tommy's strong sense of personal accountability unexpected and refreshing. Out in the free world, "rights" are usually given much more prominence than "responsibilities". I found myself thinking that Tommy's sense of personal responsibility exceeded that of the men called upon to carry out executions on people like him. So often they salve their consciences and distance themselves from their actions with statements like "We're only doing our job", and "It's nothing personal". They claim to be carrying out the will of the people, and by devising elaborate protocols and procedures to sanitize the whole dreadful business, they feel morally able to take part in the killing operation.

I spoke about it to Paul, the pastor who had known Tommy for years. He said:

> The chief objection I have to the death penalty is religious. Jesus and killing do not go together in my mind. How can disciples of one who was executed by the powers of the state be so ready to embrace the very same punishment for others? How can the message of love, forgiveness and mercy of Jesus be squared with our willingness to kill? Forgiveness and mercy should not be dispensed lightly or easily, and society has a right to protect itself from those who are truly dangerous, but executing absolutely precludes those who need such gifts from ever receiving them.

He went on to talk more specifically about Tommy:

> For me personally, there is also what we might call the "Tommy problem". I cannot conceive how anyone will be served by the execution of this man. The person who died at his hand will still be dead. Those who loved that man will still miss him. And a whole new group of people will be filled with grief and sorrow. The Tommy I know is no longer a serious threat to anyone. The punishment he has received has been more than sufficient to turn him away from the course he was on ... I have no fear that the man would again fall into the path of crime. It would be a tragedy of the highest order to execute a man long after he has gotten the message about what is precious and wonderful about human life ... Tommy has endured much. But for the life of me I cannot imagine how his execution improves our world. I can only imagine the great hurt it would cause for many of us ... Tommy is a thoughtful, concerned and caring man. Capable of loyal friendship, filled with good humour, deeply aware of his shame and his responsibility for his actions. I can honestly say that my life is better for my having known him, and he will always be my friend.

17

Giving and Receiving

I N RECENT YEARS, a great deal of research has been done into the physical characteristics of the criminal mind, as opposed to the sociological causes of criminality. Imaging of the brains of psychopaths has revealed distinct differences from the brain patterns of normal people. Doctors who work in this field have suggested that hormones such as adrenalin and cortisol can adversely affect behaviour in people with a propensity for violence. The neuro-transmitter serotonin has also been linked with increases in aggression. Some scientists believe in the existence of a gene which predisposes carriers to violent behaviour. Yet others believe that brain damage at birth or as a result of accidental injury, or the psychological damage of child abuse, can all lead to explosive, uncontrolled outbursts of anger in later life.

Some research by Danish scientists on boys born between 1959 and 1961 showed that those who were later convicted of acts of violence had several factors in common. In spite of normal scans and neural and physiological tests during the first year of life, many of them had deteriorated by the age of one: memory, verbal and visual abilities were all poor. They were also more likely to react aggressively when provoked. The study found that around 80 per cent of them had suffered problems during birth.

All this asks questions about responsibility. If someone commits murder, how responsible are they for their actions? What if they have a medical condition such as schizophrenia, a head injury or have suffered some other trauma? It would be wonderful to think that at some time in the future science might have advanced sufficiently to identify such problems and discover effective treatments. We could look forward to a time when our prisons might be virtually empty, and criminals might be treated, to repair damage. Meanwhile, however, we are left with our current solutions, which involve locking up ever more people, or disposing of them like rubbish.

Our best course of action is to get involved. People who don't concern themselves with the welfare of our prison population are on the whole those who believe that criminals have forfeited their right to be considered and heard. They believe that offenders have nothing to contribute to society. I know that isn't true. In my encounters with prisoners I have come across anger, frustration and pain – but this has been more than outweighed by warmth, humour, concern and deep regret. These are real people with hopes and fears like all of us, and my attitudes have changed since I got to know them.

How could I ever have suspected where God would take me, when I first contacted Peter all those years ago? I was looking for an answer to my questions about his actions, and having gained them, I imagined that I could go back to my quiet, confined, middle-class life. I was wrong: God likes to move us out of our comfort zones, and teach us to depend on him more. We must take risks in order to grow, but we are always held safely in his love. He knows us better than we know ourselves.

Who would choose a middle-aged English woman, a shy only child from a sheltered background, to visit the toughest of men and women in the most stressful of situations? Yet God does the unexpected. His ideas are radical, bold and unconventional. In all my contacts with prisons, I had never been afraid, never lost for words, and always "at home" in my unusual surroundings, with my unlikely friends. They in turn seem to like me and relate to me, although we appear to have no common ground. One of them once told me that many of the men and women on Death Row are totally ostracized, not only by the rest of the community, but also by their own families: "Lots of these guys have people who won't come across town to see them, yet you are prepared to travel halfway across the world to see them. That's mind-blowing!"

Would I have been likely to go down that particular road of my own accord? I think it's most unlikely. The things we want to do, and are good at, are not always God's chosen path for us. If we feel ill-equipped and have no particular wish to do something, it may well be what the Lord has in store for us! We are guaranteed an exciting and profitable time.

I realized how much I had changed when my friend Mike, who is a vicar, called me recently. One of his parishioners had been found guilty of embezzlement and was awaiting sentence. Mike had attended the trial and was convinced of Simon's innocence; he wanted to support him if at all possible. Knowing of my interest in these matters, he asked me if I had any contacts who might help. I searched out a few papers which could be useful, and Colin and I drove over to deliver them.

When we arrived at the vicarage, we were surprised to find that Simon was there. He looked shaken and distressed, and seemed glad to meet someone who could answer some of his questions about sentencing. We helped Mike by writing a character reference to present to the sentencing court, and agreed to attend with him.

On the day of the hearing the court adjourned for a coffee break, and I found myself sitting with the court correspondent from the local paper. We knew each other slightly (I had tutored his son), and he asked me why I was there. I told him I was supporting Simon.

"He's going down for a long time," he said confidently. "I've covered lots of cases like this, and fraud on that scale carries a long sentence."

Once, I would have said nothing, bowing to his experience. Instead, I found myself thinking of all the times in the past when I had failed to help someone – failed to speak out or to act as I knew I should. This time, I knew I had to speak up for Simon.

"I don't think so," I said. "We don't believe he did it. We've been praying about it, and I think he'll be all right."

At last I had had the courage of my convictions. I had finally done the right thing.

When we returned to the courtroom, the judge summed up the position – the severity of the crime was balanced by the fact that Simon had not personally profited from it; he had already lost his job and his reputation, and had suffered from other troubles such as severe illness and the loss of his wife. He was held in high regard by all his friends. Then the judge pronounced sentence: "Ten months in custody."

I was delighted: Simon would be free again in five months. My reporter friend was amazed.

"He's a lucky man," he said. "It's the shortest sentence possible."

"What did I tell you?" I replied. "That's the power of prayer."

I could scarcely believe that I was the same person, able to speak out about my faith and my belief in a person's innocence. My prison work had taught me to see God at work in the most difficult of situations.

It did other things for me too. I gained a wonderful set of friends, all of whom would have remained strangers to me without this shared concern. The people who work so tirelessly in the USA for the abolition of the death penalty do so for little financial reward. They are the "givers", without whom the world would be a poorer place. They are people who put the needs of others before their own, and are not quick to judge: "There will be no mercy for the man who has shown no mercy. Mercy triumphs over judgement" (James 2:13).

Concern for offenders is a complex issue, and we need to be aware of many elements, not least the point of view of the victim and their family and friends. Championing the outcast and unloved in society is seldom a popular thing to do. Sister Helen Prejean found this when she began to visit Patrick Sonnier, who was sentenced to death for the brutal murder of two young people. The story of their improbable and sometimes uneasy friendship formed the basis for her book *Dead Man Walking*, and the film of the same name. Sister Helen ran into trouble with the parents of the two murdered youngsters, who felt betrayed by her association with their children's killer. She met with much criticism and was forced to address their hurt and grief by meeting them face to face. She eventually set up an organization to support the victims of such crimes.

In trying to understand why people do terrible things to others, we must be sensitive to those who have suffered. While we preach forgiveness in Jesus' name to the sinner, we must never excuse the crime or forget those whose lives have been ruined. There are many bereaved and grieving people who also need Christians to comfort them in their desolation, as Sister Helen acknowledged.

So why should we bother doing this work? There are plenty of innocent people in the world who deserve our help: the old, the lonely, the many in Third World countries who suffer poverty and starvation. I know all this, and I can only say that others may be led to their work; I am doing the work that I was led to, for a cause that is unpopular and where there are considerably fewer workers. The warm welcome and acceptance which has greeted my efforts reassures me that this is the work I should be doing, and I have never doubted that it comes from God.

On looking into my own personal mirror, I have to acknowledge how far I have come since I sent off that first tentative note out of curiosity. I am not the same person with the same views and opinions as the one who made that first tremulous journey up the M6 to Liverpool. I never expected it to lead to these unlikely friendships so far from home. My eyes have been opened to a world far removed from my own cosy and protected one: the more contact I had with the prisoners, the more I realized that they mainly came from broken homes, and many of them had grown up with violence, abuse and neglect as daily occurrences. This realization changed me. Nowadays I am far less quick to judge; I am more tolerant, understanding and sympathetic – and more grateful for my own stable home and happy childhood.

Visiting America always gives me a buzz – not just because I enjoy travelling and visiting exciting new places, and not just because of the pleasure of meeting people who have become friends, but because the experience has enriched my life at so many levels. The best friendships change us for the better. It has been wonderful to make warm friendships with people who have tremendous personal qualities. Even on Death Row, which is the last place I expected to do so, I have met with integrity, reliability and care. You might expect people who are serving long prison sentences to be hardly able to bear to talk to "outsiders", yet I have seen no signs of jealousy of those of us who have our freedom.

As an only child, I have always found it difficult to

share, yet I meet with great generosity among inmates. Visitors are not allowed to take food into the prison – we have to buy snacks from the prison slot-machines. Prisoners (who have little enough cash) often give me and my daughters chocolates they have bought for us. They can "buy" the right to have Polaroid photographs taken, to send to family and friends, and I have often seen men give away the rest of their prepaid voucher to another prisoner. They are also generous with their time. Most of them spend hours reading legal documents and preparing their court cases, yet they are willing to spend time in creating art work to give away and send to friends. They pour love, care and energy into this work: it clearly gives them a thrill when their efforts are appreciated. I have learned humility by meeting prisoners who have nicer personality traits than I have myself.

It has also been great fun. As well as the adventure of travelling, I have enjoyed sharing the humour and wit of the prisoners, and our visits always involve a great deal of laughter, banter and teasing – it's very healing, as it lightens tension and breaks down barriers. Anyone who thinks Death Row is a place of deep depression has not understood the enormous zest for life among the men who know their span may be limited; they love life and they love to laugh. In visiting time, at any rate, they manage to enjoy themselves against all the odds.

I have benefited from the widening of my horizons – not only in tolerance and understanding the backgrounds of the prisoners, but through discovering the different culture of the United States. Before I started my visits to Death Row, I wasn't particularly well travelled. I found the US to be a place of many contradictions: there was the mismatch between the conservative and progressive elements in society, and the confusion that arose in my mind when I met Christians who supported the death penalty.

Previously I had very little knowledge of African American culture, but now I am delighted to be welcomed by my friends to eat with them in black restaurants and try to understand the fine distinctions of the world in which they move. Racism these days is less overt than it was thirty years ago, but there is no doubt it is still endemic in American society; by travelling with my friends I have become aware of it in a way that I could never have imagined from my cosy white world at home.

My self-esteem has been improved by feeling that I am doing something useful – an important part of my activity in the early days. It was rewarding to help others, and to have a sense of purpose at a time when my own life was less than satisfying. Since then, of course, I have realized that the friendships and contacts I have made are immensely satisfying for their own sake. Someone asked me recently if I would like to work for the Probation Service in this country, since I had such an interest in prison welfare. I had to say no. I get on well with prisoners simply because I am not part of the system, a volunteer from outside who is meeting them because I want to, not because I am paid to do so.

I have also benefited from the companionship of prisoners. When I was desperately lonely, it was wonderful to know that I had friends who cared about me; when I married Colin and had the blessing of his love and support, it was heart-warming to know how much my friends rejoiced with me.

There was a time when I imagined that I was "doing good" for people like Tommy, and perhaps I patted myself on the back a little, both emotionally and spiritually, for my "good works". I was fooling myself. Such smug attitudes were turned around on me: I quickly realized how much I was gaining from the men and women in prison. I had to learn some humility, and accept all these gifts, from the most unlikely of sources. I went expecting to give to them, but instead they gave to me. "Pass no judgement, and you will not be judged; do not condemn, and you will not be condemned; acquit, and you will be acquitted; give, and gifts will be given you. Good measure, pressed down, shaken together, and running over, will be poured into your lap" (Luke 6:37–38).

18

The Waiting Room

OVER THE YEARS I have shared deeply in the lives of my prison friends – their problems and concerns, their hopes and fears, their joys and sorrows. My own life has moved on, through a second marriage, a house move, a new church fellowship and new friends. Yet for my prison friends, very little has changed.

Roberto is still in the same prison. His hopes of release are fading, as the promised investigation into the police force that arrested him has ground to a halt. His wife Regina still writes to him faithfully, but she cannot afford to visit him very often. She works hard at three part-time jobs, trying to get the money together for her next fare to America.

There is better news of Tommy: he has been granted leave to appeal against his sentence. If he is fortunate, and if he manages to get some adequate representation, there is a chance that his sentence may be commuted – from the death penalty to life imprisonment. We hope and pray that the shadow of execution will be lifted from him.

I was thinking about this on my most recent visit to Riverbend Maximum Security Facility. I had been in the waiting room there many times. As I waited for a female prison officer to come and conduct the compulsory body search, I glanced idly around. On the notice-board was a display of photographs, showing the development of the new prison from the date when work began, after the old facility, The Walls, was condemned. There was a picture of the footings being dug, the walls rising, the roof going on. It was clear that the State of Tennessee was proud of its new high-tech facility, equipped with the latest in electronic monitoring, back-up systems and anti-escape devices.

I had been present on several occasions when the governor had been conducting tours, and heard him telling the visiting legislators and politicians about the prison – a modern, innovative solution to the problem of housing and managing the least desirable and most troublesome citizens. He was keen to showcase it as an example to other, less enlightened states.

Alongside the photograph display was a plan of the entire complex, with each block labelled and numbered. Tucked away behind the larger buildings was a small, unimportant-looking one, which simply bore the title "Building 8". I knew what it was, and it chilled me: this was the execution chamber, the embodiment of the failure of the entire system. This was where those prisoners on Death Row ended their lives. It was the final end which awaited many of the people I knew – people who were warm, funny, lonely, guilty, remorseful, and hopeful – in other words, human.

I was waiting for a few minutes, looking forward to seeing my friends, and after my visit I would be free to leave. They were waiting until the state made its decision – to kill or reprieve. Their wait could last for the rest of their lives.

The door opened and the guard arrived: "How y'all doin'?" she asked brightly.

Useful Addresses

LifeLines
PO Box 347
Darlington
DL3 6WZ
email: lifelines.secretary@ntlworld.com
website: www.lifelines.org

Justice
59 Carter Lane
London
EC4V 5AQ
Tel: 020 7329 5100
email: admin@justice.org.uk
website: www.justice.org.uk

Amicus
Assisting Lawyers for Justice on Death Row
199 Strand
London
WC2R 1DR
Tel: 0870 414 1000
email: admin@amicus-alj.org
website: www.amicus-alj.org

The Liberty Christian Trust
PO Box 3212
Cumbernauld
Glasgow
G67 4WG

Amnesty International
99–119 Rosebery Avenue
London
EC1R 4RE
Tel: 020 7814 6200
email: info@amnesty.org.uk
website: www.amnesty.org.uk

Death Penalty Information Center
website www.deathpenaltyinfo.org